# Royal Air Force Bombers

Of World War Two                                    Volume Two

by Philip J. R. Moyes

illustrated by James Goulding

Doubleday & Company, Inc., Garden City, New York

© Philip J. R. Moyes, 1968
© James Goulding, 1968

## Available in the same series

| | |
|---|---|
| American Fighters | Volume I |
| German Air Force Fighters | Volume I |
| Royal Air Force Bombers | Volume I |
| German Air Force Bombers | Volume I |
| Royal Air Force Fighters | Volume I |
| Japanese Navy Bombers | |
| German Air Force Fighters | Volume II |
| American Fighters | Volume II |
| German Air Force Bombers | Volume II |

Series Editor. C. W. Cain

First published in England, 1968
by Hylton Lacy Publishers Limited.
Coburg House, Sheet Street, Windsor,
Berkshire, England

Doubleday & Company, Inc.,
First Edition 1969  Second Edition 1971

Printed in England by Mears Caldwell Hacker Limited, London

# Foreword

AT no time has the interest in aircraft of World War Two been as great as it is today. Already many books have been published in this country on the main combat planes of the period, Allied and Enemy alike, and scale-model aircraft kits are equally numerous. Yet the enthusiasts everywhere seem to be demanding more information on this absorbing subject every day.

The most frequent plea is for information about the operational histories of World War Two aircraft rather than merely their development histories, because the latter have, in many cases, already been recorded adequately. Coupled with this is an ever-increasing demand for colour illustrations of the subjects described—and indications are that this requirement is by no means confined to modellers, for many non-"kit bashers" apparently derive great pleasure from seeing famous aircraft of yesteryear recreated by a skilful artist.

It is in an attempt to meet these two present-day requirements that this series of books, *Men and Machines,* is being produced, the present volume being the second of three which will collectively cover all the Royal Air Force bomber aircraft of World War Two. Other volumes will deal with Royal Air Force fighters of the same period and also the wartime aircraft of the other major powers.

Much of the information in this series is completely new, and all of it—whether it be narrative or artwork—is fully authenticated. This second volume describes six separate types of aircraft, ranging from the Vickers Wellesley single-engined bomber (which, to quote Mr. James Goulding, who well remembers their first public appearance at the 1937 Hendon Air Pageant, "resembled sailplanes rather than bombers") to the really purposeful-looking Handley Page Halifax four-engined bomber. None of the aircraft in this volume could be called outstanding in so far as their war records go—and indeed it is probably true to say, in some cases, that any successes they were involved in were achieved in spite of their qualities rather than because of them! To be fair, though, aircraft were frequently misemployed in wartime and expected to perform tasks for which, for one reason or another, they were totally unsuited.

In keeping with the theme *Men and Machines,* the main emphasis in this volume is again on action and atmosphere. The adoption of this new slant is quite deliberate and, judging by the general response to Volume One, it is welcomed.

As before, James Goulding has spared no effort to ensure the accuracy and authenticity of his illustrations and there can be no doubt that he has produced the finest drawings of the aircraft in question ever to have been published.

London, 1968

PHILIP J. R. MOYES

# Contents

*Colour Illustrations*

# Boeing B-17C Fortress I

Initially designed for a purely defensive role—the protection of the American coastline from foreign surface fleets—the Boeing B-17 shared the honours with the Consolidated Liberator of being the principal heavy bomber of the U.S.A.A.F. in World War II. The prototype, the Model 299, was designed to an Army Air Corps specification of 1934, and it was the aircraft's defensive role, and not its seemingly formidable defensive armament concentrated in five fuselage stations, that suggested the name 'Flying Fortress'. The 299 was powered by four 750 h.p. Pratt and Whitney Hornet engines, and in August 1935—only a month after its roll-out—it flew to Wright Field, Dayton (Ohio), averaging 232 m.p.h., a record-breaking performance for those days. Thirteen service test models were subsequently built, and the last one, delivered in January 1939, was the first to be specially modified for high-altitude bombing and fitted with turbo-superchargers.

First production model was the B-17B, this being followed in 1940 by the B-17C, which featured a long bath-shaped ventral gun position, and had sliding windows over the waist gun positions instead of blisters. Twenty B-17Cs were bought by the British Purchasing Commission and the first of these Fortress Is, as they became known in R.A.F. service, were ferried across the Atlantic in the spring of 1941. The first aircraft to arrive was AN521, which landed at Prestwick in the early hours of April 14 (Easter Sunday), having made the crossing from Gander, Newfoundland, in the record time of 8 hr. 26 min.

Following 'processing' at the maintenance unit at Burtonwood, the Fortresses were supplied to 90 Squadron, which, after having served as an operational training unit in the early months of the war, had been re-formed in 2 Group for the express purpose of operating the American bombers in the high-altitude day-bombing role. From the outset the scheme was a tragic failure and No. 90's ill-advised technique of operating the Fortress Is by day at heights up to 35,000 ft., and furthermore doing so mostly on individual sorties, brought forth strong criticism from the Americans, one of whom eventually summed-up the whole sad story thus:

'In the fall of 1940 a number of Boeing B-17Cs were transferred from Langley Field to Wright Field to be refitted for service in England. They were refitted with self-sealing tanks and 50-calibre guns. All the guns were hand-held and the sighting equipment rudimentary. . . . There was no tail gun position. In the spring of 1941 these ships were ferried to England. We gave the British specific instructions that these 'planes were to be used for training purposes.

'I was in England when the 'planes arrived. We explained to the British our doctrine for the use of the 'planes. We told them that the crews had to be well-trained, that a crew should drop 200 practice bombs before attacking a real target; that the 'planes were designed to fly in formation for protective purposes; and that by using them as trainers, trained crews could be ready to operate the new, properly equipped Fortresses when we delivered them. For some reason, which only the British understand, they decided to use the 'planes offensively.

'Number One ran off the runway upon arrival in England, smashed the landing gear, and never flew again. While it sat there it was "cannibalised"— a part taken off here and a part there until the ship was picked clean as a Thanksgiving turkey.

'Number Two was sent over Brest to take a crack at the *Scharnhorst* and was so badly chewed up by enemy action that it disintegrated like the one-hoss shay upon landing at Plymouth.

'Number Three was burned from pure carelessness.

*The Fortress I in close-up showing the bomb-aimer's panel in the nose.*

'Numbers Four, Five and Six were flying in formation over Narvik, Norway, when they were set upon by Nazi fighters. All of them were lost. One apparently landed intact in Norway and it probably gave the Germans their first look at the American bombsight.

'Number Seven took a gallant American to his death, Lieutenant Bradley, testing equipment in the upper reaches of turbulent air currents and fast-

*The crew of 90 Squadron's Fortress I AN523 'D-Dog' board their aircraft at Polebrook in July 1941. [I.W.M.*

forming ice when something happened. The sole survivor was the squadron medico.

'Number Eight was turned over to the R.A.F. experimental laboratories and continues its career as a guinea-pig.

'Number Nine dove out of the clouds one day at about 1,000 ft. and continued straight into the ground.

'The remainder were then withdrawn from active operations and sent to the Middle East for employment within their limitations. We knew they were not combat worthy for we had been able to build only a few experimental models. . . .'

The official records of 90 Squadron show that the

*Below: One of the R.A.F.'s twenty B-17Cs flies over the U.S. on an air test prior to delivery to Britain in 1941. The prefix letters 'AM' were originally applied to all the R.A.F. B-17Cs in error but these were soon changed to the correct letters 'AN' and on delivery the aircraft became known as Fortress Is.*

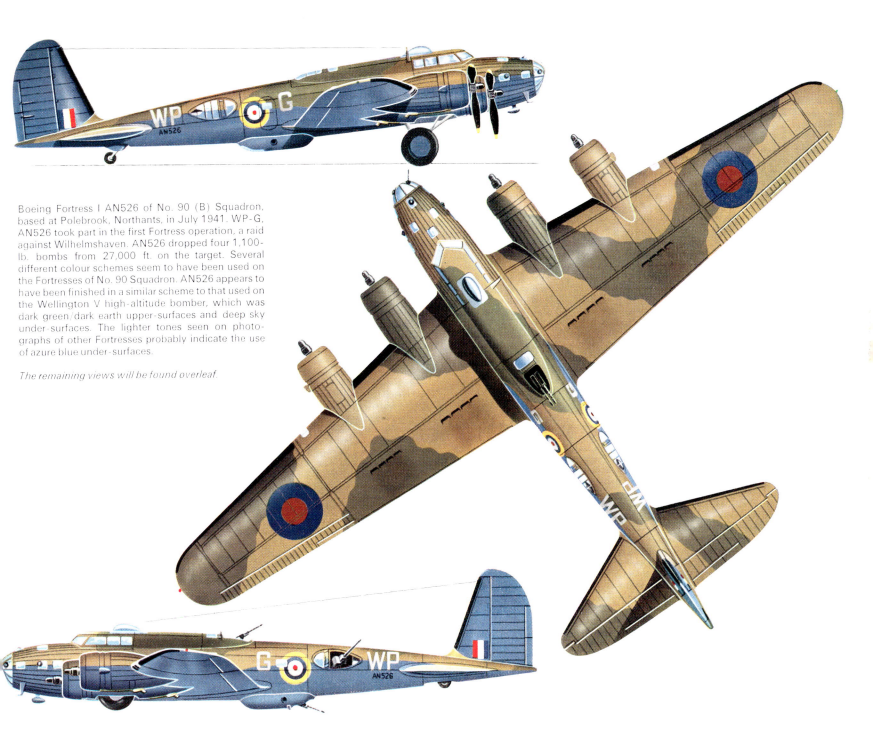

Boeing Fortress I AN526 of No. 90 (B) Squadron, based at Polebrook, Northants, in July 1941. WP-G, AN526 took part in the first Fortress operation, a raid against Wilhelmshaven. AN526 dropped four 1,100-lb. bombs from 27,000 ft. on the target. Several different colour schemes seem to have been used on the Fortresses of No. 90 Squadron. AN526 appears to have been finished in a similar scheme to that used on the Wellington V high-altitude bomber, which was dark green/dark earth upper-surfaces and deep sky under-surfaces. The lighter tones seen on photographs of other Fortresses probably indicate the use of azure blue under-surfaces.

*The remaining views will be found overleaf.*

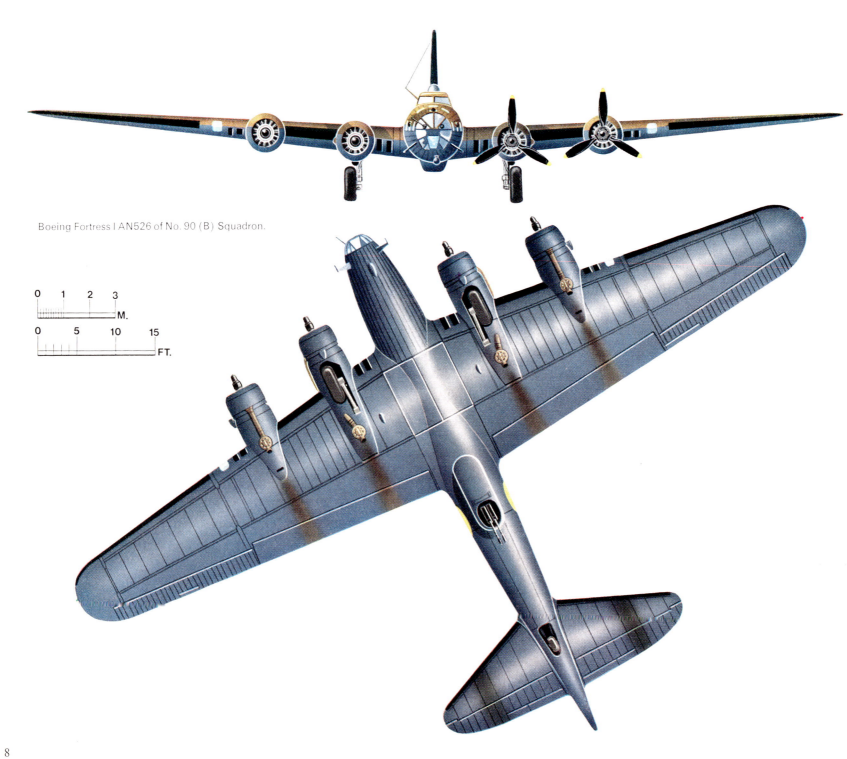

Boeing Fortress I AN526 of No. 90 (B) Squadron.

0 1 2 3
M.

0 5 10 15
FT.

Bristol Blenheim I L1283 of No. 90 (B) Squadron, based at
Bicester, Oxon., in October 1938. TW-H, L1283, is shown
here in typical markings of the Munich Crisis period.

*The remaining views will be found overleaf.*

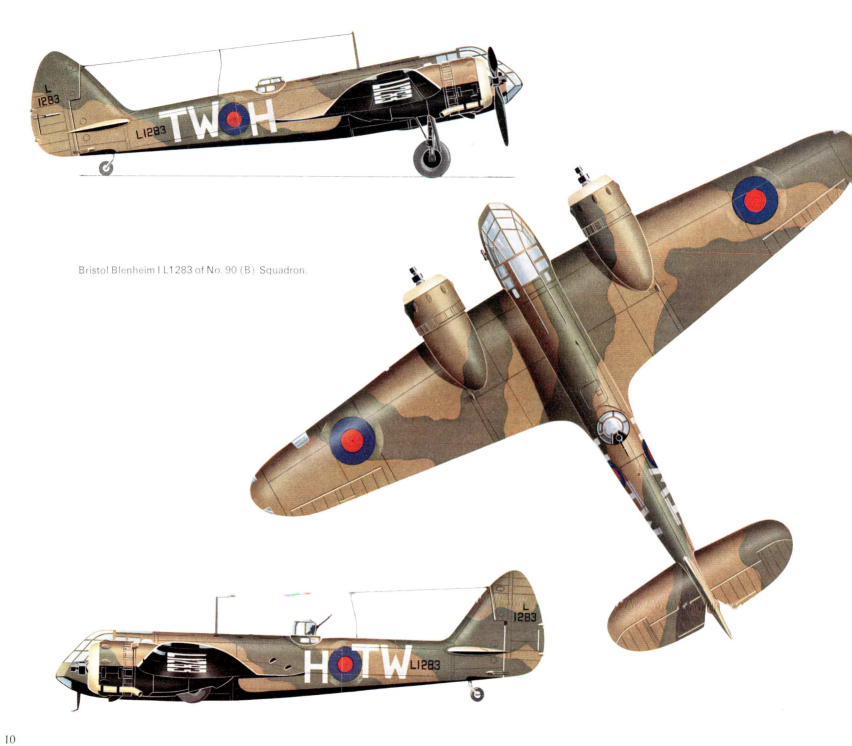

Bristol Blenheim I L1283 of No. 90 (B) Squadron.

*Fortress I AN521 runs up its engines in the summer of 1942. This particular machine was, on Easter Monday 1941, the first of the R.A.F.'s B-17Cs to arrive in England.*

foregoing remarks are more or less perfectly true. The squadron received its first Fortresses early in May 1941 at Watton (Norfolk), and by the end of May (by which time the unit was based at West Raynham and flying from the satellite airfield at Massingham) five were on charge and the task of working-up was well underway. Because the Fortresses boasted such hitherto unheard-of refinements as carpeted and padded cockpits and built-in ashtrays, they quickly became known as 'gentlemen's aircraft'—until the rigours of operational high-altitude flying shattered the illusion.

The men chosen to fly the Fortresses needed to be experienced, no older than 24 years of age, and all had to pass a decompression test of four hours at an equivalent of 35,000 ft. As relatively few people were able to fly at that height and work on oxygen alone in an unpressurised aeroplane, crews had to be recruited from many squadrons. The first crew-members came from 115 Squadron (Wellingtons) and were two Englishmen, one Canadian and one New Zealander. Because the Fortresses' side gun ports had to be open on operations, the temperature inside the bombers fell to extremely low levels, sometimes as low as minus 50° Centigrade. Crew members sometimes suffered from decompression sickness, coughing, intense itching and fainting, and these troubles were never to be overcome.

On June 4, the C.O. of 90 Squadron (W/Cdr J. MacDougal) and his crew, in order to allow the wireless, intercom and oxygen equipment to be tested at extreme altitude, took a Fortress up to 38,000 ft. 'This height was reached in 40 minutes', wrote the squadron diarist, 'and they were still climbing at 500 ft. per minute.' Later that month Fortress AN522 (F/O Hawley) iced up badly at 33,000 ft. during a height test, went into a terminal velocity dive and broke up, the wreckage falling at Catterick Bridge, some 10 miles north of Catterick, Yorks. As the bomber plummeted earthwards the crew were pinned down by excessive *g*, but one of the two medical officers aboard was thrown

*Centre, right: This air-to-air view of AN526 shows to advantage the Fortress I's 'bathtub' accommodating the ventral gunner. AN526, as 'WP-G' of 90 Squadron, was on July 8 1941, the first R.A.F. Fortress to drop bombs on the enemy.*

*Right: AN523 'D-Dog' takes-off from Polebrook in the summer of 1941. On August 16 1941, this particular machine was destroyed in a forced landing at Roborough aerodrome, near Plymouth, after sustaining serious battle damage. [I.W.M.*

*A Fortress I makes a low pass over the airfield at Polebrook (Northants) in the summer of 1941.*

clear. Tragically, he lacked sufficient oxygen even to pull the parachute ripcord. Another medical officer, F/Lt Steward, A.F.C., from the R.A.E., Farnborough, who was in the rear part of the fuselage, which fell more slowly than the other piece, was able to bale out at a height believed to have been about 12,000 ft. and make a safe parachute descent. He was the sole survivor.

Towards the end of June the squadron moved to Polebrook, Northants, and on July 3 another Fortress was written off. This one—AN528—met its end when one of its engines caught fire while being run-up, with the result that the aircraft was burned out. Five days later the squadron finally began operations. Three aircraft took part—AN526 'G' (W/Cdr MacDougal), AN519 'H' (S/Ldr MacLaren) and AN529 'C' (P/O Mathieson). Briefing was at 13.00 hr. and the target was announced at Wilhelmshaven. A stick of four 1,100-lb. American bombs was to be dropped by each aircraft across the target, the centre of which was the U-boat building-yard. The three aircraft were detailed to go out in open formation and attack from 27,000 ft., afterwards climbing to 31 or 32,000 ft. to make their getaway. P/O Mathieson reached the target, dropped his four bombs across the centre of it and returned without incident. W/Cdr MacDougal dropped two bombs on the target but the remaining two hung up. Another run-up was made but again the bombs failed to leave the aircraft. MacDougal then

turned away and made a further attempt to drop the two bombs on the Frisian Islands, but to no avail; he then returned to base. MacLaren had engine trouble at 20,000 ft. while climbing on the outward journey, oil leaking from the breather valves of all four engines. At 27,000 ft. oil was spurting out and freezing on the tailplane one inch thick. The gunners reported severe vibration, the Fortress refused to climb any higher, and as oil pressure was falling badly MacLaren decided to bomb targets in the Frisians and return to base. A town on Norderney was selected for attack but all bombs missed. MacLaren then turned for home, but soon after having done so the Fortress began to vibrate so violently that the wireless operator's morse key disintegrated. The vibration continued for 14 minutes. 12,000 ft. were lost in the first four minutes and broad band I.F.F. (Identification Friend or Foe) was switched on. When the Fortress was down to 4,000 ft. the tailplane became free of oil and the vibration ceased; the aircraft then continued to base.

None of the crews saw any flak on this mission but the C.O.'s crew, at 32,000 ft. and 40 miles north of Terschelling, reported two enemy fighters, believed to be Bf. 109s, 2,000 ft. below them. The fighters climbed and approached on the starboard beam, closing to about 600–800 yds., when one of them appeared to go into an involuntary spin, and was still seen spinning about 600 ft. below. The second fighter broke off the

*Airmen of 90 Squadron point out some of the finer details of the Fort's tail to two members of the Army.*

attack and followed the first one down. No fire was exchanged.

In the weeks that followed this inauspicious start No. 90's Fortresses flew 23 more high-altitude day-bombing missions. These were far from successful, for out of a total of 48 sorties flown in the course of the missions, no less than 26 were completely abortive i.e. no bombs whatever were dropped either on the primary targets or on the alternatives*). There were numerous reasons for this sad state of affairs, but the main ones—and they are mentioned time and again in the official raid reports—were (1) the Fortress's guns and gun-mountings tended to freeze up at altitude; (2) their turbo-superchargers failed at altitude; (3) ten-

* The only targets that the Fortresses did claim to have attacked besides Wilhelmshaven were Brest, Emden, Kiel, Borkum, de Kooy, Cologne, Speikeroog, Rotterdam and Oslo.

tenths cloud frequently covered the selected target areas; and (4) the aircraft sometimes encountered conditions of temperature at operational altitude which resulted in their leaving tell-tale vapour-trails.

Thus it was that after September 25 1941 no further raids were attempted with the Fortresses in the European theatre, 90 Squadron's flying activities being confined mainly to training, although it also co-operated with Messrs. Warner Brothers, who were making the film *Flying Fortress*. The squadron disbanded in February 1942 and a survey of its aircraft losses in Europe since May 1941 shows that, all told, three were lost on operations and four more in non-operational flying and ground accidents.

Although there is no doubt whatever that the Fortress I's defensive armament was inadequate, it is wrong to aver, as several writers have done when

writing about the aircraft, that 90 Squadron found this a serious handicap from the outset; the reason being that no air combats took place until the 10th operation—a raid on Brest on August 16. On that day two aircraft attacked the German battle-cruisers *Scharnhorst* and *Gneisenau*. One machine dropped its bombs from 35,000 ft. and returned home without incident, but the other (AN532 'D'), after bombing from 32,000 ft., was engaged by seven enemy fighters, and in a 23-minute running battle, fought all the way down to 8,000 ft, and suffered serious damage. Two gunners were killed early in the fight (another died later) and not until the crippled Fort was thirty miles

*A fine study of AN530 'F-Freddy' of 90 Squadron in October 1941, when the squadron had finished ops from the U.K. and was 'starring' in the Warner Bros. film* Flying Fortress. [*Charles E. Brown.*]

from the English coast did the enemy fighters withdraw. The captain, P/O Sturmey, nursed the bomber back to England, crossed the coast at a mere 600 ft. and attempted a forced-landing at Roborough aerodrome, near Plymouth, but the machine overshot, caught fire and was destroyed.

The only other occasion when a U.K.-based Fortress of 90 Squadron was attacked by enemy fighters was on September 8, when four of the bombers, operating from Kinloss on detachment from Polebrook, attempted to bomb the German pocket-battleship *Admiral Scheer* in Oslo harbour. On this occasion three Fortresses were lost. AN525 'D' was attacked by two Bf. 109s over Norway and is believed to have shot one of them down before being shot down itself; AN535 'O', after having also been attacked by fighters, limped home on two engines, crash-landed at Kinloss and was destroyed by fire; and AN533 'N' took off ten minutes after the others and was not seen again. The fourth aircraft abandoned its mission owing to 10/10 cloud in the target area and returned to base without incident.

In the autumn of 1941 four of 90 Squadron's Fortresses were sent to Shallufa in the Suez Canal Zone of Egypt, whence, at the outset, night bombing raids were made on Benghazi, the target chosen for the first daylight raid. The range of the Forts at the required altitude proved insufficient for the operation and over the target the bombs which hung up had to be literally kicked from the racks. It will be remembered that hang-ups had first been experienced by No. 90 during the Wilhelmshaven raid on July 8. At that time various experiments had been made with the Fortress's bomb release gear. The usual load of four

American 1,100-pounders were individually held in place by a webbing strap, one end of which was attached to the aircraft and the other to the electromagnetic release unit. This latter was one of the items of equipment which continually suffered from icing and it was found advisable to station a member of the crew on the catwalk during the bombing run so that he could kick off any bombs that stuck fast.

During a sortie against a target near Tobruk on November 8, AN529 (P/O Swanson) ran out of fuel and force-landed in enemy territory. As it was impossible to set the machine on fire to prevent its capture by the enemy, the crew destroyed the Sperry bomb-sight with .303 in. gunfire before being rescued by members of the Rifle Brigade. On the same day AN518 also ran short of fuel on the return trip but managed to reach Mersa Matruh safely.

Soon fighter opposition forced a change in targets and so raids were mounted against shipping. On one such sortie AN518 was engaged by two Bf. 109s which, to the surprise of the fighters, the bomber easily out-turned.

No. 90 Squadron in the U.K. disbanded on February 12 1942, by which time the Middle East detachment had become part of 220 Squadron. Maintenance in the desert proved extremely difficult and matters were not improved when AN521 was destroyed in a crash after an engine had caught fire during a fuel consumption test. Very soon after this incident operations ceased, and although a few Fortress Is were subsequently used for general reconnaissance (by 220 Squadron based in the U.K.), the type was not used again operationally in the straight bomber role.

If nothing else, the operational career of the B-17C in R.A.F. service enabled the Americans to remedy many of the shortcomings revealed in aircraft and tactics before U.S.A.A.F. crews were required to take the Fortress into action. When the Eighth Air Force

*A waist gunner with one of the Fortress's six .50 in. calibre Browning machine-guns. When the Forts first arrived in Britain, all the .50 in. cal. guns were 'beefed up' to give a rate of fire of 900 rounds a minute. A seventh gun in the Fort was a .303 in. Browning—referred to by the crews as 'the pea shooter' to distinguish it from its bigger brothers.*

began operations in Europe in late 1943 the B-17E was its standard equipment, but even this did not prove to be really battleworthy, so an even better model was introduced—the B-17F, with which the U.S. daylight high-altitude bombing concept was pioneered. Next—and indeed the most famous version, as every schoolboy knows—was the B-17G, best all-round American heavy bomber of World War II. Quantities of B-17Fs and 'Gs were supplied to Britain under Lease–Lend, and some of them, redesignated Fortress II and III respectively, were supplied to Bomber Command for use in the bomber support (radio countermeasures) role by 100 Group. This, however, is another story, and outside the scope of this present work.

*AN532 'J-Johnny', one of the four Fortresses that eventually served with 90 and 220 Squadrons' detachments in the Middle East in 1942. [I.W.M.*

## Specification

Fortress I: *Crew* 6; *power plant* four 1,200 h.p. Wright Cyclone R-1820 G-205A; *span* 103 ft. 9½ in.; *length* 67 ft. 10½ in.; *wing area* 1,486 sq. ft.; *empty weight* 31,150 lb.; *loaded weight* 45,470 lb.; *max. bomb load* 4,000 lb.; *max. speed* 325 m.p.h. at 28,000–30,000 ft.; *service ceiling* 35,000 ft.; *range* 2,000 miles with max. bomb load; *armament* one moveable .303 in. m.g. in nose, twin .50 in. m.g. in dorsal and ventral positions, plus two .50 in. m.g. in beam positions.

# Bristol Blenheim

First of the high-speed twin-engined all-metal aeroplanes to join the R.A.F., the Bristol Blenheim, was developed from the Bristol Type 142 six-passenger high-speed transport built in 1934–35 for Lord Rothermere, the newspaper proprietor, who wanted an aeroplane to rival the fast American airliners then coming into use. Type 142 first flew in April 1935 and very soon aroused such great interest in Air Ministry circles on account of its high performance—it clocked more than 300 m.p.h. during airworthiness acceptance trials at Martlesham—that Lord Rothermere generously presented it to the nation, having already named it 'Britain First'.

A joint Air Ministry/Bristol design conference was held in July 1935 to discuss the question of converting Type 142 into a bomber, the outcome being the issue by the Air Ministry of Specification B.28/35 which Bristol met with Type 142M—the Blenheim I; this was very similar in layout to the civil transport, the main difference being that the wing was raised from the low to the mid-position to provide for a bomb bay in the fuselage below the wing spars. Armament comprised a single Browning gun in the port wing and a similar gun in a semi-retractable dorsal turret.

The Air Ministry ordered Blenheims straight off the drawing board as part of the R.A.F. Expansion Scheme. The initial contract for 150 was placed in September 1935 and the 'first off', K7033, served as the prototype, making its maiden flight at Filton, Bristol, on June 25 1935. Deliveries to home-based squadrons began in March 1937 (beginning with 114 Squadron at Wyton, Hunts), the Blenheims replacing such interim equipment as the Hawker Audax, Hawker Hind and Avro Anson. Further contracts were placed from July 1936 onwards (including some for export)

*Blenheim Is of 114 Squadron—K7038 'D' nearest the camera —circa 1937. ['Flight International'.*

*A trio of Blenheim Is of 62 Squadron—L1131, L1108 'W', and L1113 'Z'—on a training sortie from Cranfield (Beds) early in 1938. ['Aeroplane'.*

*A Mk. I of 90 Squadron is refuelled at Bicester during the Annual Air Exercises in August 1938. ['Aeroplane'.*

and before production switched to the Mark IV in 1936, a total of 1,280 Mk. Is had been built, nearly half of them by A. V. Roe at Chadderton and Rootes Securities at Speke and Blythe Bridge. At the time of the Munich crisis the Blenheim I equipped seventeen R.A.F. bomber squadrons at home—in Nos. 1, 2 and 3 Groups, but during the ensuing months they were supplanted by Blenheim IVs, or by other types of aircraft. The Blenheim I entered service overseas in January 1938—with 30 Squadron in Iraq. Early in 1939 it entered service in India. At the outbreak of war, in September 1939, only two home-based bomber squadrons were still equipped with the Mk. I but overseas it equipped eleven squadrons in Egypt, Aden, Iraq, India and Singapore. (Also seven home-based fighter squadrons had converted, or else were in the process of converting to a fighter adaptation, the Blenheim IF; but that is another story.) The Blenheim—Mks. I, IF and IV—was the most numerous type on R.A.F. charge at the outbreak of war, the total held being no less than 1,089.

Blenheim Is saw active service in France (with 18 and 57 Squadrons of the Air Component of the B.E.F.), the Middle East (including Egypt, Libya, Greece and Crete) and finally in Malaya where, during the Japanese invasion they fought valiantly against overwhelming odds until—as in Greece and Crete—they were virtually wiped out. In the Middle East, on June 11 1940, the type gained the distinction of being the first R.A.F. aircraft to bomb the Italians in World War II: 26 Blenheim Is of 45, 55 and 113 Squadrons made a dawn bombing and strafing attack on the Italian airfield at El Adem, Libya, No. 55 leading. Three aircraft failed to return. The attack was repeated later in the day and in all 18 enemy aircraft was destroyed or damaged on the ground.

In the Far East a V.C. was won by a Blenheim I pilot—S/Ldr A. S. K. Scarf of 62 Squadron. This was a posthumous award and was not made until after the war because only then did the details of his gallantry become known. The official citation tells the story:

'On 9th December, 1941, all available aircraft from the Royal Air Force Station, Butterworth, Malaya, were ordered to make a daylight attack on the advanced operational base of the Japanese Air Force at Singora, Thailand. From this base the enemy fighter squadrons were supporting the landing operations.

'The aircraft detailed for the sortie were on the point of taking off when the enemy made a combined dive-bombing and low level machine-gun attack on the airfield. All our aircraft were destroyed or damaged with the exception of the Blenheim piloted by Squadron Leader Scarf. This aircraft had become airborne a few seconds before the attack started.

'Squadron Leader Scarf circled the airfield and witnessed the disaster. It would have been reasonable had he abandoned the projected operation which was intended to be formation sortie. He decided, however, to press on to Singora in his single aircraft. Although he knew that this individual action could not inflict much material damage on the enemy he, nevertheless, appreciated the moral effect which it would have on the remainder of the squadron, who were helplessly watching their aircraft burning on the ground.

'Squadron Leader Scarf completed his attack successfully. The opposition over the target was severe and included attacks by a considerable number of enemy fighters. In the course of these

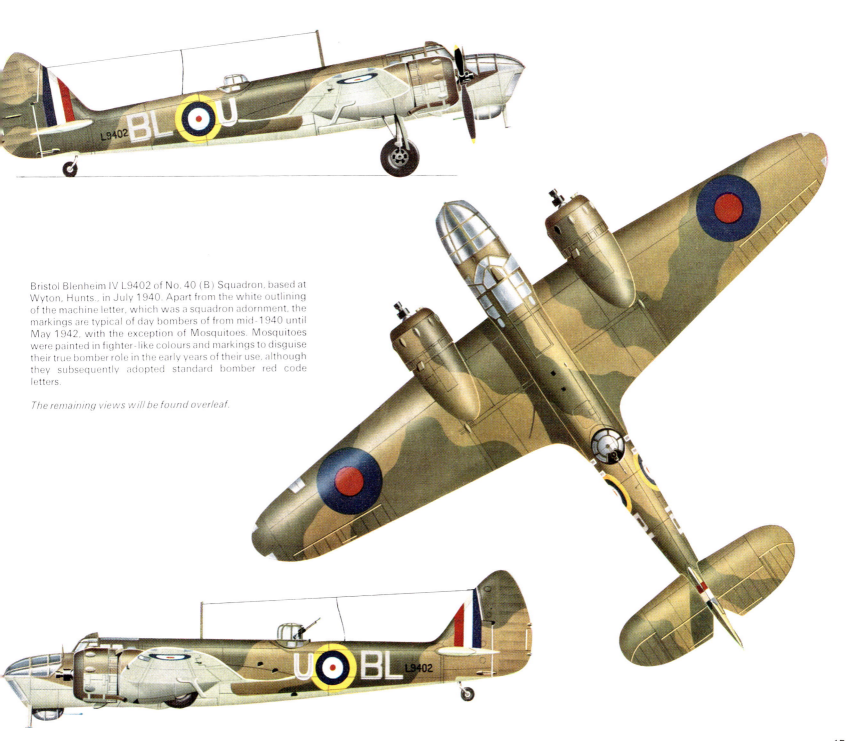

Bristol Blenheim IV L9402 of No. 40 (B) Squadron, based at Wyton, Hunts., in July 1940. Apart from the white outlining of the machine letter, which was a squadron adornment, the markings are typical of day bombers of from mid-1940 until May 1942, with the exception of Mosquitoes. Mosquitoes were painted in fighter-like colours and markings to disguise their true bomber role in the early years of their use, although they subsequently adopted standard bomber red code letters.

*The remaining views will be found overleaf.*

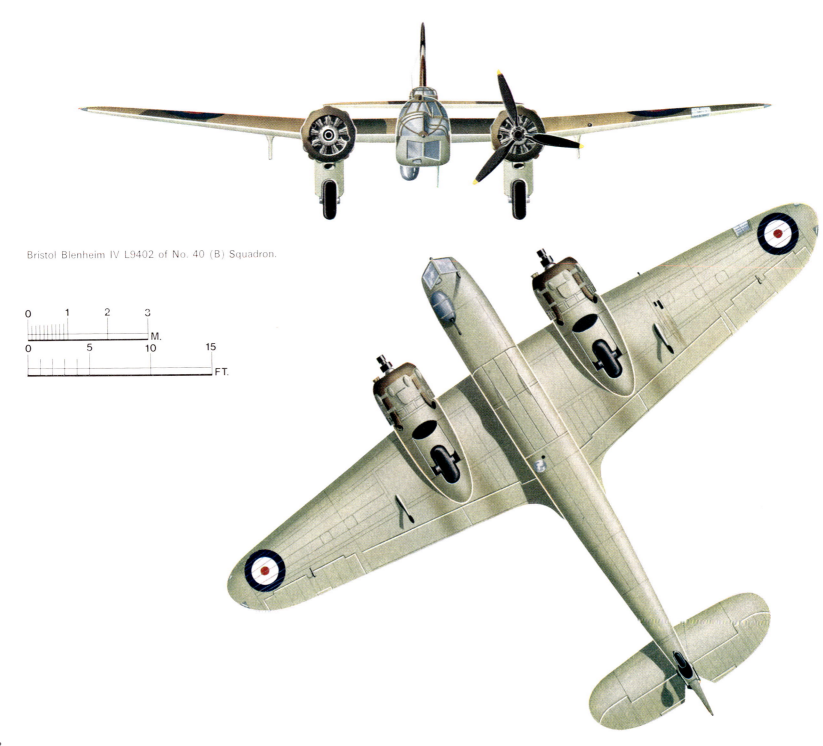

Bristol Blenheim IV L9402 of No. 40 (B) Squadron.

0  1  2  3
M.
0  5  10  15
FT.

*An early production Blenheim IV, L4842, banks steeply to port during a test flight from Filton, Bristol, early in 1939. ['Flight International'.*

encounters, Squadron Leader Scarf was mortally wounded.

'The enemy continued to engage him in a running fight, which lasted until he had regained the Malayan border. Squadron Leader Scarf fought a brilliant evasive action in a valiant attempt to return to his base. Although he displayed the utmost gallantry and determination, he was, owing to his wounds, unable to accomplish this. He made a successful forced landing at Alor Star without causing any injury to his crew. He was received into hospital as soon as possible but died shortly after admission.

'Squadron Leader Scarf displayed supreme heroism in the face of tremendous odds and his splendid example of self-sacrifice will long be remembered.'

The Blenheim IV, which entered production early in 1939, differed from the Mk. I in having its nose extended by three feet to accommodate the navigator ahead of the pilot and below his line of sight, Mercury XV engines instead of Mercury VIIIs, and additional fuel tanks in the outer wings to extend its range to 1,900 miles. Production was again shared by the parent company, Avro and Rootes Securities, and at the time of its entry into service early in 1939 it was the fastest bomber in the world. When war came the Mk. IV equipped seven first-line squadrons of

*Ground crew carry light bombs to a Blenheim of either 11 or 113 Squadron at Ma'aten Bagush in the Western Desert circa August 1940. [I.W.M.*

A Blenheim IV of 139 Squadron lands at an R.A.F. airfield in
France after a reconnaissance sortie over the Siegfried Line
during the winter of 1939–40. [I.W.M.

Bomber Command and on the first day of hostilities
the first aircraft to cross the German frontier was a
Blenheim IV (N6215) of 139 Squadron, Wyton
on a photographic-reconnaissance sortie. Next day,
as a follow-up to this mission, Blenheim IVs of 110 and
107 Squadrons attacked enemy warships in the Schillig
Roads, near Wilhelmshaven, in what was the R.A.F.'s
first bombing raid of the war. Leading the raid (and
first to drop his bombs) was F/Lt K. C. Doran of
110 Squadron, in N6204, who for his work that day
subsequently gained one of the first two awards made
to any member of the British Services in World War II
—a D.F.C., which was gazetted at the same time as
a similar award to F/Lt A. McPherson who had
flown the 139 Squadron photo-reconnaissance sortie
on September 3.

Two Blenheim IV squadrons (114 and 139 from
Wyton) went to France in December 1939 to join the
Advanced Air Striking Force. Early in 1940 some
Mk. IVs were issued to 18 and 57 Blenheim I bomber
squadrons which had been in France since September
1939 as part of the Air Component of the B.E.F., and

*Mk. IVs of 40 Squadron prepare to leave Wyton on a mission
in July 1940. Note the light bomb carriers beneath their
fuselages aft of the bomb bay. [I.W.M.*

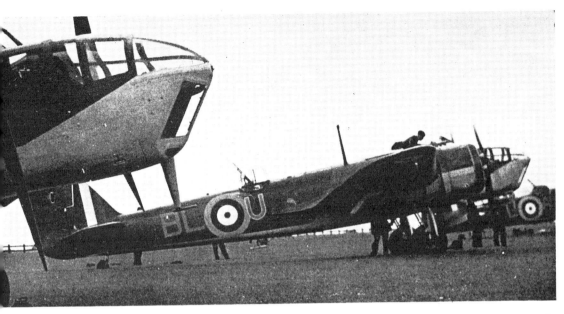

Blenheim IVs of 2 Group were likewise embroiled in the ill-fated campaign and they, too, suffered heavy losses. The reason for all these losses, of course, was that the Blenheim was totally incapable of defending itself when attacked by fighters. Its armament, comprising a single forward-firing .303 inch gun and two guns of similar calibre in a dorsal turret was virtually useless. One of the blackest episodes of all at this time was on May 17, when twelve machines of 82 Squadron (Watton, Norfolk) were ordered to attack German columns near Gembloux. A few miles from the target, the Blenheims, flying in two formations of six, met intense and very accurate flak. The first burst of fire brought down one machine and the formation began to open out. Fifteen Bf. 109s then closed in and only one of the original twelve Blenheims survived the battle, and even that one was badly damaged. Only the exceptional determination of the squadron commander, W/Cdr the

In May 1940 all four squadrons shared in the hopeless task of trying to stem the German Army's advance into the Low Countries and France. They all suffered heavy losses both in men and machines, and No. 18's experiences are typical. On May 10, when the *blitzkrieg* began, two out of three machines despatched on reconnaissance sorties failed to return. The next day two more crews and three aircraft were lost. Scarcely a machine returned from any sortie undamaged. Sgt A. Thomas, piloting L8863, a Mk. IV, was shot through the neck, the bullet passing out through the opposite jaw. Despite the pain and loss of blood from his wound he managed to fly the aircraft back to base, but he subsequently died. On the 17th, ten bombing sorties were flown against German armoured columns, but two more Blenheims were lost. The same day the squadron was ordered to withdraw to Guyancourt. Only two aircraft were left behind, and these were rendered unusable. Next morning six aircraft attacked enemy armour, and all returned safely. Later that day came another withdrawal, this time to Crécy; but by mistake the Blenheims landed—with the sole aid of two petrol-tin flares—at Abbeville. Three more unserviceable machines were left behind at Guyancourt.

The badly-mauled squadrons withdrew to England at this stage and eventually re-mustered with new Blenheim IVs in 2 Group. Meanwhile, the U.K.-based

*Blenheim IVs of 101 Squadron fly in Vic formation, with T1825 'Y-Yoke' leading, on a sortie from Oakington (Cambs) circa August 1940.* [Charles E. Brown.

*Another view of Mk IV T1825 'SR-Y' of 101 Squadron, circa August 1940. [Charles E. Brown.*

biography *Mission Completed*—a rear-firing K gun in the stern and in each engine nacelle.

Following the fall of France, 2 Group's Blenheims attacked Hitler's growing concentrations of invasion barges and small ships in the North Sea and Channel ports. Attacks were also made on fringe targets, and sometimes the Blenheims operated by night. Towards the end of 1940 enemy airfields were high on the priority list in order to relieve Britain from incessant night bombing. Daylight shipping attacks began in March 1941, the technique being for a formation of Blenheims to fly low over the sea and, as soon as enemy ships were sighted, to split up and attack their selected victims from mast height. This was extremely hazardous work, for apart from the inevitable barrage of deadly light flak, there was the ever-present danger that the aircraft would strike the masts of a vessel and, indeed, this happened on several occasions when pilots misjudged their height. Delayed-action bombs were used in these attacks, the Blenheim's usual load being four 250-pounders or two 500-pounders with four 25-lb. incendiaries. A particularly good day's work was done on March 31 when W/Cdr S. C. Elworthy (who is now Air Chief Marshal Sir Charles Elworthy, and a former C.A.S.), C.O. of 82 Squadron (Watton), led a formation of six aircraft to attack shipping off Le Havre. Two tankers, escorted by flak ships, were sighted, and Elworthy went for one of the tankers. He scored a direct hit and set the vessel on fire. The second

*A Blenheim IV of 18 Squadron sweeps over Holland towards the target on July 16 1941, during 2 Group's daring low-level attack on German shipping in Rotterdam docks. [I.W.M.*

Earl of Bandon, prevented the temporary disbandment of the squadron. Within forty-eight hours, in fact, Bandon had scraped together enough crews and new machines to lead six aircraft on a night operation.

In an attempt to reduce Blenheim losses the aircraft's armament was augmented during the summer of 1940 by the addition of a rear-firing K gun in a blister under the nose emergency hatch. Earlier in the year some squadrons had in fact improvised extra gun installations, and one of these, a free nose-mounted Vickers K gun, later became an official modification with the gun mounted in a gimbal. Among the other local lash-ups were the Blenheims of 107 Squadron with—as Sir Basil Embry mentioned in his auto-

Morley and Great Massingham) against the dock area at Bremen on July 4. The Blenheims went in low through the balloon barrage and under high-tension cables to attack from chimney-top level, and one machine actually brought back telephone wires trailing from its tail wheel. A hail of flak greeted the bombers and four were shot down and most of the others seriously damaged. W/Cdr H. I. Edwards, 105 Squadron's C.O., won the Victoria Cross for his leadership in this raid; his aircraft was Blenheim IV V6028 'D-Dog'.

In face of mounting losses and a serious shortage of Blenheims, the 2 Group squadrons were withdrawn from attacks on shipping in the North Sea at the end of October 1941. Some units were then temporarily transferred to Malta, whence they harassed shipping plying between Sicily and the North African ports.

Meanwhile, following the German invasion of Russia, Bomber and Fighter Commands' so-called *Circus* operations were intensified to divert enemy fighters from the Eastern front. No. 2 Group's Blenheims duly made massed escorted daylight raids against heavily-defended key targets, one particularly notable *Circus* being that against the power stations at Knapsack and Quadrath, near Cologne, on August 12 1941, when 54 Blenheims from six squadrons were

despatched. A week later during a *Circus* against a power station at Gosnay, Blenheim IV R3843 'F-Freddy' of 18 Squadron, Manston, called *en route* at St. Omer to drop a pair of artificial legs to fighter ace W/Cdr Douglas Bader, who had been shot down and captured shortly beforehand.

From the winter of 1941–42 the Blenheim IV was supplanted in 2 Group by the Boston and in the summer of 1942 one of the group's last Blenheim units was re-armed with the Ventura.

In addition to operating in Europe, the Blenheim IV served overseas from early 1941. Space does not permit a detailed account of its work overseas to be given, but it can be said that it rendered sterling service in the Middle East (including, not only the main desert fighting, but also the two side-shows in Syria and Iraq) in the defence of Ceylon and, finally, in the Burma campaign. It was withdrawn from use as a bomber in the Middle East in January 1942 but in the Burma theatre (where it first made its appearance in January 1942) it soldiered on until 1943. The squadrons that flew Mk. IVs against the Japanese in Burma were Nos. 11, 34, 42, 60 and 113; their Blenheims operated from bases in India, Burma and, in one instance, China (for a short while). Last squadron to operate the Blenheim was No. 11, whose aircraft were based

*Two 500-lb G.P. bombs await delivery to the enemy by a Blenheim IV of 2 Group in the summer of 1941.*

tanker was also hit by bombs from another aircraft and left burning. Although considerable flak was thrown up by the escort vessels, the Blenheims escaped with only minor damage. On the same day Sgt I. Overheu, R.N.Z.A.F., of 21 Squadron, scored a direct hit on one of two destroyers escorting a convoy off the Frisian Islands. Two weeks later, when his squadron intercepted another convoy in the area and claimed hits on two merchantmen and one of the escorts, Overheu was responsible for the damage to one of the larger ships. During this attack two of the six Blenheims taking part were shot down, but Overheu survived. Three months later his aircraft hit the mast of the vessel he was attacking and crashed into the sea.

Raids were also made on the enemy's North Sea and Channel ports, one of the more spectacular of these missions being that carried out by twelve Blenheims of 105 and 107 Squadrons (Swanton

*Blenheim IV V5899 'GB-J' of 105 Squadron lands at Swanton Morley (Norfolk) in 1941.*

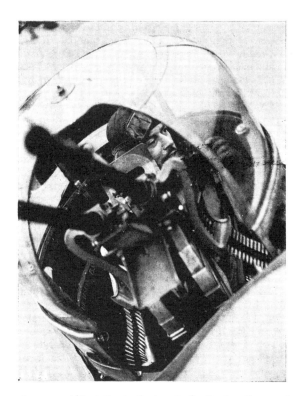

*A gunner at his station in the turret of a Bomber Command Blenheim IV circa October 1941.*

throughout the 1943 monsoon on the wet airfield of Feni (Bengal), attacking chosen points through which the Japanese were bringing supplies to their Arakan front from Rangoon.

'So old were these aircraft now, and so excellent was the squadron spirit', says the Short Official History of the Burma campaign when describing the events of that period, 'that it was said the Blenheims flew on happiness alone. The ground crews were devoted to their aircraft, sometimes working for forty-eight hours, with hardly a pause, to repair a Blenheim in time for an operation, and then seeing it take off, circuit and return with the same old trouble. Blenheim spares were still unobtainable, and only by the ground crews' knowledge of the idiosyncrasies of each engine were they made to go at all. "It'll clear in the air" began as a hopeful catch-phrase and ended as a squadron battle-cry. Within the squadron the Australian and British personnel teamed up into

*A Blenheim V, or Bisley as it was known in the R.A.F., is prepared for operations at an airfield in North Africa in 1943. [I.W.M.*

"Pig Islanders" and "Pommie Bastards", and by these affectionate names they were known. As so often, when conditions were at their worst the contentment was greatest; the comradeship of the Blenheim crews became famous enough in India for men to try to get themselves posted to the Blenheims, despite the maturity of the aircraft.'

For the record, the final Blenheim IV sortie was flown on July 31 1943, when twelve aircraft (with 25 Australians out of a total crew strength of 36) bombed Myingyan railway station.

Meanwhile, in 1942 the Blenheim V, or Bisley as it was known by the R.A.F., entered service. This version 942 examples of which were built (by Rootes at Blythe Bridge), differed from the Blenheim IV chiefly in having a redesigned nose, increased armour protection, an improved dorsal turret (Bristol B.X) and Mercury XXX engines. It was issued in the late summer of 1942 to 13, 18, 114 and 614 Squadrons which were then in Army Co-operation Command. These squadrons were posted to North Africa in November 1942 in connection with Operation *Torch* and, operating as part of the Tactical Bomber Force, initially from Blida, outside Algiers, made daylight raids, notably against the docks and airfields of far distant Tunis and Bizerta. Losses were heavy—partly due to the Bisley's poor performance*—and they were soon forced to operate by night. At the end of November the Bisleys

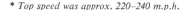

* *Top speed was approx. 220–240 m.p.h.*

*Armourers bring a trolley load of 250-lb. G.P. bombs to a Blenheim IV of 2 Group at an English airfield in January 1942.*

were ordered forward to Canrobert for close-support work. They operated from Souk-el-Arba advanced landing ground and were engaged in the Chouigui area where the First Army was holding on desperately. Casualties were very high, largely owing to the absence of fighter cover, and on December 4, 18 Squadron was virtually wiped out. After two attacks in the morning against an enemy landing ground near Chouigui, the

C.O., W/Cdr H. G. Malcolm, led nine Bisleys against the same target during the afternoon. As the bombers approached the target area at 1,000 feet they were intercepted by fifty to sixty Bf. 109s. Not one of the Bisleys returned. For his determination in trying to fight his squadron through to its objective and back to base, Malcolm was posthumously awarded the Victoria Cross—the thirteenth V.C. won in the air in World War II, and the only air V.C. awarded during the entire campaign in North Africa. His name was commemorated in the R.A.F. Malcolm Clubs, the first of which opened some months later in Algiers.

After the events of December 4, the Bisleys were employed almost exclusively on night interdiction, and some very effective work was done on moonlight nights, mostly against transport on the roads leading to Sfax and Tunis. Casualties were gratifyingly low.

The Bisleys gave way to Bostons in the early months of 1943, but during the period March to August of that year the type saw further action as a bomber in the Burma theatre when it was operated by Nos. 34, 42 and 113 Squadrons. The final operational sortie by Bisleys was a raid against Japanese targets at Kudaung and Laundaung on August 15 1943, by aircraft of 113 Squadron (Feni), which had converted to Bisleys from Blenheim IVs in late 1942.

Above: Medical equipment is unloaded at a forward area from an R.A.F. Bisley of a squadron operating from India. [I.W.M.

Below: Operational flying shots of Bisleys are rare. This one shows two aircraft on an offensive patrol over Japanese-occupied Burma early in 1943. Although the Bisley was better armed than the Blenheim IV it was slower and unpopular with its crews. [I.W.M.

## Specification

Blenheim I (Mk. IV data in parentheses where different): *Crew* 3; *power plant* two 840 h.p. Bristol Mercury VIII (two 920 h.p. Bristol Mercury XV); *span* 56 ft. 4 in.; *length* 39 ft. 9 in. (42 ft. 7 in.); *wing area* 469 sq. ft.; *empty weight* 8,100 lb. (9,790 lb.); *loaded weight* 12,500 lb. (13,500 lb.); *max. bomb load* 1,000 lb. (1,000 lb. internally, plus 320 lb. externally); *max. speed* 266.5 m.p.h. at 11,800 ft. (266 m.p.h. at 11,000 ft.); *service ceiling* 27,280 ft. (22,000 ft.); *range* 920 miles with max. bomb load (1,460 miles with 1,000 lb. bomb load); *armament* one fixed .303 in. m.g. forward and one .303 in. m.g. in dorsal turret (one fixed .303 in. m.g. forward and one or two .303 in. guns in dorsal turret plus—sometimes—twin .303 in. guns in blister beneath nose and single fixed rearward-firing .303 in. m.g.s in engine nacelles).

# Handley Page Hampden

Together with the Armstrong Whitworth Whitley and the Vickers Wellington, the Handley Page Hampden bore the brunt of the R.A.F.'s bombing offensive in the early part of World War II, and like its stablemates it was then still classed as a 'heavy' bomber. Stemming from a specification issued in mid-1932 (B.9/32, from which the Wellington also stemmed), it was faster than the Whitley or Wellington and represented a compromise between these aircraft and the Blenheim both in terms of speed and payload/range performance.

Specification B.9/32 called for a twin-engined day bomber of appreciably higher performance than any previously envisaged, and to meet it, Dr. G. V. Lachman, Handley Page's chief designer, conceived what was for that time an extremely radical aeroplane —yet one which clearly owed much to his earlier H.P.47 general-purpose monoplane prototype to

G.4/31—centred on the new and promising Rolls-Royce Goshawk steam-cooled engine. When the latter proved to be a failure the Bristol Perseus became favourite but the final choice was the Bristol Pegasus P.E.5S(a), forerunner of the Pegasus XVIII.

The new bomber was allotted the company designation H.P.52, and the prototype, serialled K4240, made its first flight on June 21 1936, at Radlett. A distinctive feature of the machine was its very slender fuselage— flat-sided and deep at the front and terminating in a tapered tail boom. This saved weight and also enabled the four crew members to be brought together in a compact group. And, incidentally, it led to the production aircraft being given such nicknames as the 'flying suitcase', the 'flying tadpole' and the 'flying panhandle'. However, the arrangement eventually proved to have one serious drawback: the cockpit was

so narrow that if the pilot was killed or badly wounded it was impossible for any other member of the crew to pull him from his seat and take over—even if only to keep the machine on an even keel while everyone baled out.

Within six weeks of the prototype H.P.52's first flight, the Air Ministry placed an initial production order for 180 H.P.52s to Specification B.30/36. At the same time it ordered 100 H.P.53s—H.P.52s powered by 24-cylinder H-type Napier Dagger engines; these aircraft were subcontracted to Short and Harland at Belfast and eventually became known as Herefords. A second prototype, H.P.52, L7271, flew early in 1937. G.-R. Volkert was now Handley Page's chief designer (for the second time in his career), Dr. Lachman having returned to his first love—technical research—and he adapted L7271 to become the H.P.53 prototype, which latter made its maiden flight on July 1 1937, from Boscombe Down. L7271 was later supplied to Shorts as the pattern aircraft for the Hereford Mk. I.

The production prototype H.P.52, L4032, flew in May 1938. This machine had new rounded Perspex nose incorporating an optically flat bomb-aiming panel, and the dorsal gun position was fitted with a domed cupola which was hinged to allow it to be pushed back over the gunner's head. Power plant was the 980 h.p. Pegasus XVIII.

Production Hampdens began to leave the assembly lines in the summer of 1938 and in September deliveries commenced to 5 Group of Bomber Command, first squadrons to receive the type being Nos. 49 and 83, both of which were fully equipped by the end of the year, with a third squadron, No. 50, in the process of re-equipping. Meanwhile the English Electric Company at Preston had been given the go-ahead to build an initial batch of 75 Hampdens under sub-contract, while in Canada a consortium of several prominent financial organisations and firms known as Canadian Associated Aircraft had received an initial order for 80 Hampdens for the R.A.F.

At the outbreak of war in September 1939, a total of 212 Hampdens were on R.A.F. charge. Ten squadrons of 5 Group were flying the type, including six first-line squadrons, two squadrons acting as O.T.U.s and two operational reserve squadrons. Early operations were against German naval units but,

*Hampdens of 144 Squadron make a formation flight from their base at Hemswell (Lincs) circa May 1939.*

*View from the dorsal gunner's position of a Hampden of three more aircraft in line astern formation.* [*I.W.M.*

results were not observed. All six machines returned safely to base.

From December 18 Bomber Command tacitly abandoned the belief that Hampdens (and Wellingtons) could operate by day in the face of German fighter opposition and thenceforth it only employed them on night operations.

The Hampdens were now switched to helping the Whitleys of 4 Group to defend our shipping from the menace of the magnetic mine which the *Luftwaffe* had been laying round the English coast since October. As the British Government would not allow Bomber Command to attack targets on land at this time, the only way in which our bombers could be used against the *Luftwaffe*'s mine-laying seaplanes was to bomb the flare-paths on the water from which these machines operated. In all, 71 continuous 'security patrols' were flown by 5 Group's Hampdens—with no aircraft missing—and the operations definitely reduced the minelaying seaplanes' activities.

Meanwhile the Whitleys of 4 Group had, since the outbreak of war, been making nightly excursions deep into Germany to drop nothing more than propaganda leaflets, or *Nickels*, on the civilian population. The Wellingtons of 3 Group were gradually brought into this unsatisfactory work, and from March 6 1940, 5 Group's Hampdens were ordered to join them on night reconnaissance/*Nickelling* flights over probable

generally speaking, such attacks as were made proved to be ineffective. They were also highly dangerous, as was clearly seen on September 29, when eleven Hampdens of 144 Squadron from Hemswell were detailed to search part of the Heligoland Bight to within sight of the German coast. On this occasion the aircraft were split into two sections—a section of five led by W/Cdr J. C. Cunningham, the C.O., and a section of six led by S/Ldr W. J. H. Lindley. Cunningham's section left Hemswell at 4.50 p.m. and was not heard from again; it was apparently destroyed by enemy fighters from the North Frisian Islands. Lindley's section found two enemy destroyers in the search area steaming in line astern at 20 knots, and prepared to attack from a height of 300 ft. Owing to the destroyers' manœuvres and flak umbrella, however, only three Hampdens were able to attack and the

*A Vic of three Hampdens of 106 Squadron on a sortie from Finningley (Yorks) in April 1940. Their serials and codes are L4192 'ZN-K', P1320 'ZN-B' and 'ZN-F', and one of them (P1320) is the subject of the five-view colour painting on pages 30 and 31.* ['*Flight International*'.

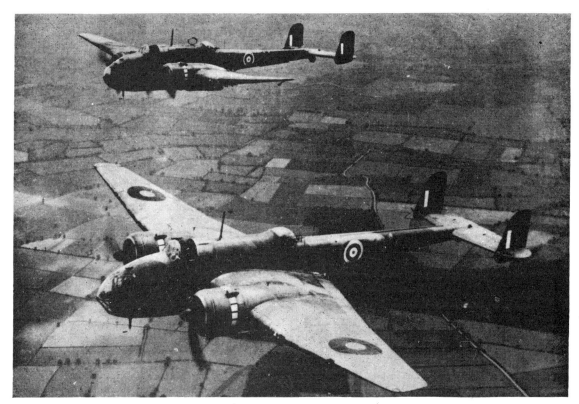

AE257 'X-X-Ray' and AE202 'K-King' of 44 Squadron in September 1941. Note the fixed Browning guns in the aircrafts' noses. [I.W.M.

targets in Germany. Between that date and the end of 1940 the Hampdens flew 123 night sorties with leaflets at a cost of one aircraft missing.

The R.A.F.'s sea-mining campaign began during the first winter of the war and it was 5 Goup's Hampdens that pioneered it. For although minelaying was held to be the duty of Coastal Command the Hampden proved to be the only aircraft available and able to carry the Mk. I modified naval mine—our first magnetic mine—although soon afterwards Beauforts of Coastal Command and Albacores of the Fleet Air Arm joined in.

The first British magnetic mines were laid off the coast of Denmark by Hampdens from 44, 49, 50, 61 and 114 Squadrons on the night of April 13–14 1941, a few days after the German invasion of Norway. The aim of the R.A.F.'s mine-laying campaign was to lay the weapons in areas unapproachable by our own ships and also to 'freshen up' existing minefields with new mines. The original minelaying, or *Gardening*, areas were the coastal waters of Denmark and Norway, but eventually the work spread along the entire enemy-occupied coast as far as Lorient. Between April 1940

and the end of that year 1,209 minelaying sorties were flown by 5 Group's Hampdens, 703 mines were laid, and 21 aircraft were reported missing on these operations—a casualty rate of less than 1.9 per cent of sorties, which was considered very satisfactory for work which, although undoubtedly much less dangerous than operating over Germany, was by no means easy.

During the Norwegian campaign Hampdens were again operated by day, and again they quickly proved to be 'easy meat' for enemy fighters. The grimmest episode was on April 12 when seven Hampdens from 44 Squadron and five more from 50 Squadron tried to attack a German warship in Kristiansand South. The twelve bombers were caught by hostile fighters which made beam attacks and hacked the formation down from the wing man inwards until half their number, including four from 50 Squadron, had perished. P/O M. G. Homer flying No. 44's Hampden L4074, had a very lucky escape indeed: a cannon shell fired by an attacking Bf. 109 went through the astro hatch only six inches behind his head and left the fuselage without exploding.

The plain facts behind these and earlier losses were, of course, that the Hampden was still a most feebly armed aircraft. It had but a single gun on top and another one underneath manned by a gunner in a hopelessly cramped position, together with two guns in front, one of which, being fixed, was completely useless. Drastic action following the losses on daylight raids in the spring of 1940 resulted in the bomber's movable rear armament—limited in traverse though it was—being doubled; this was done outside normal Service channels, and in a very short time-span by 'Bomber' Harris (then A.O.C.-in-C. of 5 Group), Group Captain E. A. B. Rice, and the 'typically English "family" firm' Alfred Rose and Sons of Gainsborough, Lincolnshire, and an amusing account of it all can be found in Sir Arthur Harris's well-known work, *Bomber Offensive*.

On March 16 the *Luftwaffe* dropped bombs on British soil for the first time (the island of Hoy in the Orkneys), killing a civilian. Three nights later, on March 19–20, Whitleys and Hampdens of 4 and 5 Groups of Bomber Command made a retaliatory raid on the minelaying seaplane base at Hörnum on the Island of Sylt, the first British air attack on a land target in World War II. The raid lasted six hours, the first four hours being allotted to the Whitleys and the remaining two to the Hampdens. Of the 20 Hampdens participating, fifteen claimed to have attacked the target, three failed to locate it, and two returned early with engine trouble.

The Germans launched their attack on the Low Countries on May 10 1940, and on the night of May 11–12 Hampdens participated in the first big bombing attack on the German mainland—against lines of communication in and near several towns on the invading enemy's route to southern Holland. After the French collapse the so-called invasion ports received top priority on Bomber Command's target list, and again the Hampdens of 5 Group played a full part. It was the practice of the group to allot each port to a squadron, and each basin to a crew. As a result the crews not only learned their particular targets very well, they were also infused with a keen spirit of competition, each one trying to destroy more barges than any other. Among the Hampden crews operating at that time was F/O (as he then was) Guy Gibson, later to win the V.C. on the famous dam-busting raid in May 1943. He was in 83 Squadron in 1940 and has described in his book, *Enemy Coast Ahead*, how flying round Antwerp docks during a particularly heavy raid on September 15–16

*Close-ups of the dorsal and (right) ventral gunners' positions in a Hampden. [Left photo 'Aeroplane'.*

*The floor of Sgt. John Hannah's 83 Squadron Hampden after the mission against the invasion barges at Antwerp in which he won the Victoria Cross. [I.W.M.*

he 'could easily see the tanks on board, the guns on mountings at the stern of each invasion craft, the tarpaulins over sinister objects on the docks'. As we now know it was Bomber Command's raids on the invasion ports in concert with the more widely publicised activities of Fighter Command during what came to be known as the Battle of Britain, that finally led Hitler, on October 12 1940, to 'postpone *Sealion* (the invasion of Britain) until the spring of 1941'.

It was during the Antwerp raid which Guy Gibson described that Sgt John Hannah, an 18-year-old wireless operator/air gunner in another 83 Squadron Hampden, won the V.C. His aircraft, serial number P1355, was subjected to intense flak over the target and received a direct hit from a shell which apparently burst inside the bomb bay. Flames quickly enveloped both Hannah's and the rear-gunner's compartments, and as both fuel tanks had been holed, there was grave risk of the fire spreading. Hannah forced his way through the blaze to get two extinguishers and found that the rear gunner had been compelled by the fire to leave the aircraft. He could have done likewise, through the bottom escape hatch or forward through the navigator's hatch, but he chose to stay and fight the fire, though thousands of rounds of ammunition were exploding in all directions; he was almost blinded by the intense heat and fumes, but had the presence of mind to obtain relief by turning on his oxygen supply. He used up the two extinguishers and then beat out the flames with his log book. The great inrush of air through the large holes caused by the shell made the bomb bay an inferno, and much of the duralumin sheet on the floor of Hannah's station was melted away, leaving only the cross-bearers. Hannah's face and eyes

were badly burned but when at last the fire was out, he crawled forward. He then discovered that the navigator had also been driven to bale out and passed the latter's log and maps to the pilot, who brought the

*Interior view of the Hampden. ['Aeroplane'.*

Hampden safely back to base. The aircraft had a hole in the fuselage large enough for a man to crawl through. The rear gunner's cockpit and half the interior of the fuselage were charred ruins. There were holes in the wing and fuel tanks.

Strategic bombing of Germany was begun in May 1940, the first raid being made on the night of 15th–16th, when 99 bombers were despatched to attack oil and railway targets in the Ruhr. The offensive was continued without intermission and among the various transport bottlenecks attacked during the summer of 1940 was the Dortmund–Ems canal. This canal was of particular importance in the German communication system, as it formed one of the main outlets to the sea for Ruhr coal and manufactures, and at the point where it was carried across the river Ems by two aqueducts it was particularly vulnerable. Aware of the weak spot, the enemy did his utmost to defend it with flak batteries, but this did not deter our bomber crews, and after several attacks, including a particularly successful one by 24 Hampdens of 61 and 144 Squadrons from Hemswell, photo-reconnaissance at the end of July showed that the newer of the two aqueducts had been severely damaged; part of the canal had been drained making it impassable to traffic at this point. On August 12–13 ten Hampden crews of 49 and 83 Squadrons who had been specially trained in moonlight low-level techniques over the Lincolnshire fens were despatched from Scampton to attack the older branch of the canal. Actually five Hampdens created a diversion by attacking adjacent lock gates and river craft, while the remaining five attacked the aqueduct whose anti-aircraft guns were disposed so as to form a lane down which attacking aircraft were forced to fly if they wanted to reach their target. The Hampdens, carrying delayed-action bombs, went in from the north at two-minute intervals, the moon shining in the faces of the crews and throwing their objective into relief. Two of the first aircraft were shot down, the other two being badly hit. The fifth Hampden, P4403 (which, incidentally, carried a Walt Disney 'Pinnochio' emblem on its nose), captained by F/Lt R. A. B. Learoyd of 49 Squadron, dived to 150 feet through the storm of flak. Learoyd afterwards recalled how:

'After a moment, three big holes appeared in the starboard wing. They were firing at point-blank range. The navigator continued to direct me on to the target. I could not see because I was blinded by the glare of the searchlight and had to keep my head below the level of the cockpit top. At last I heard the navigator say "bombs gone"; I immediately did a steep turn to the right and got away, being fired at heavily for five minutes. The carrier pigeon we carried laid an egg during the attack.'

In addition to the holes in the wing, the hydraulic system was shot away so that neither flaps nor undercarriage would work. Realising this, Learoyd, after struggling back to base, waited for the dawn and landed without injury to his crew. Learoyd's attack seriously injured the Dortmund–Ems canal: it caused a block so serious that no boats could be passed through the canal for ten days. For his courage and gallantry in this raid, Learoyd was awarded the Victoria Cross; he was the first Bomber Command flier to receive the decoration.

On the night of July 1–2 1940, 83 Squadron became the first Bomber Command unit to drop a 2,000-lb. bomb on the enemy.* The 2,000-pounder (Semi-Armour Piercing) was dropped by Hampden L4070 captained by F/O Guy Gibson during a raid on the German battle cruiser *Scharnhorst* lying in dry dock at Kiel. The 'big stick' left the racks too late, in the last of six dive-bombing attempts made from 6,000 feet in bad visibility, and fell in the centre of Kiel town.

Production of the Hampden by the parent company ceased in July 1940, with the 500th aircraft, but prior to this deliveries from English Electric had commenced, the first Preston-built machine, P2062, flying on February 22 1940. In all, English Electric built 770 Hampdens—albeit not all as straight bombers, some being torpedo-bombers—the last leaving the line on March 15 1942.

The first Canadian-built Hampden flew on August 9 1940, and by the following October fifteen aircraft were leaving the assembly lines per month. These aircraft were ferried to Britain and total Hampden

*Ground crew prepare 500-lb. bombs and (right) a 2,000-pounder for loading into Hampdens of 61 Squadron at Hemswell in early 1941.*

* This weapon was first used operationally by Coastal Command on May 7 1940 when a Beaufort of Coastal Command dropped one near a German cruiser anchored off Norderney.

*Home again. The crew of an 83 Squadron Hampden leave their aircraft after a sortie in the summer of 1940.*

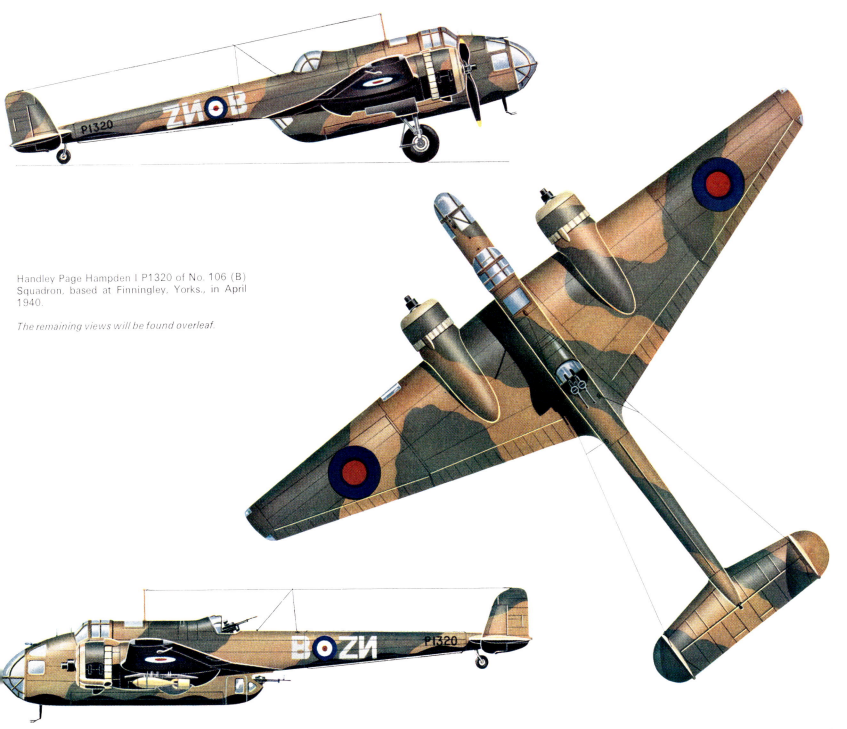

Handley Page Hampden I P1320 of No. 106 (B) Squadron, based at Finningley, Yorks., in April 1940.

*The remaining views will be found overleaf.*

Handley Page Hampden I P1320 of
No. 106 (B) Squadron.

0  1  2  3
|||||||||||||
M.

0     5    10    15
|   |   |   |
FT.

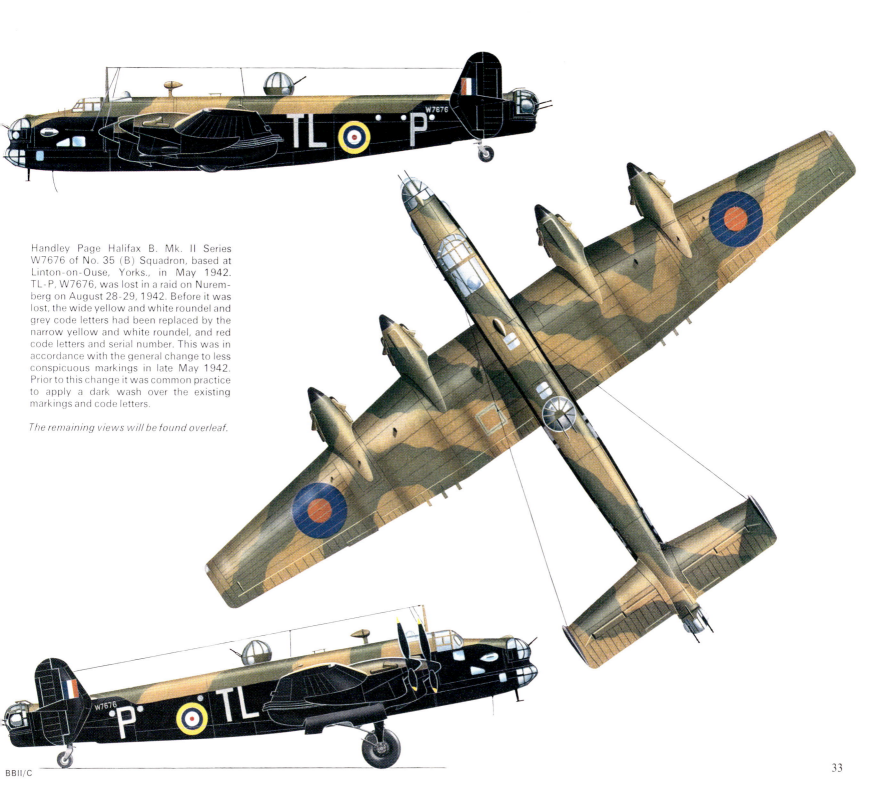

Handley Page Halifax B. Mk. II Series W7676 of No. 35 (B) Squadron, based at Linton-on-Ouse, Yorks., in May 1942. TL-P, W7676, was lost in a raid on Nuremberg on August 28-29, 1942. Before it was lost, the wide yellow and white roundel and grey code letters had been replaced by the narrow yellow and white roundel, and red code letters and serial number. This was in accordance with the general change to less conspicuous markings in late May 1942. Prior to this change it was common practice to apply a dark wash over the existing markings and code letters.

*The remaining views will be found overleaf.*

Handley Page Halifax B.
Mk. II Series W7676 of
No. 35 (B) Squadron.

*Fine study of Hampden P5304 'L-Love' of 16 O.T.U.*
*[Charles E. Brown.*

production by Canadian Associated Aircraft reached 160 machines before production ceased at the end of 1941. At one stage it was proposed that Canadian-built Hampdens be fitted with 1,100 h.p. Wright Cyclone GR1820-G105A engines, but this scheme fell through. However, in 1940 two Hampdens, L4032 and X3115, were experimentally fitted with Cyclones, and these became known as H.P.62 Hampden IIs. The Preston-built X3115 served with 415 Swordfish Squadron, R.C.A.F., from August 1942 until June 1943, but during that time it is believed to have had Pegasus engines.

The night of August 25–26 1940 saw Hampdens, in company with Whitleys, make the R.A.F.'s first bombing raid on Berlin, while on December 16–17 the 'Flying Suitcases' shared in another historic first—Bomber Command's first 'area' attack against an industrial target (Mannheim).

In the spring of 1941 much of Bomber Command's effort was diverted from the campaign against German industries in order to intervene in the Battle of the Atlantic: Attacks were made on the *Scharnhorst* and *Gneisenau*—'Salmon' and 'Gluckstein' to the bomber crews—which, after successful forays in the Atlantic had returned to Brest. The *Scharnhorst* moved to La Pallice, nearly 250 miles farther south, in July. Both vessels, plus the cruiser *Prinz Eugen*, which was now

with the *Gneisenau* in Brest, were continually attacked by Bomber Command, and on July 24 Hampdens temporarily returned to the day-bombing role when, in conjunction with a force of Wellingtons and three Fortresses, they operated against the warships at Brest. In this attack the bomber force was estimated to have scored six hits on the *Gneisenau*. Two Hampdens were lost.

After this Bomber Command gained some respite from its persistent raids on Brest, but in December 1941, when it was considered that the warships were rapidly becoming seaworthy, another heavy daylight raid was mounted although this time Hampdens did

not take part. Three days before, however, on December 13, three Hampdens of 44 Squadron were detailed to lay mines in broad daylight and without fighter escort in the mouth of the harbour at Brest, as a precaution against possible attempts by the *Scharnhorst* (which had long been back in Brest), *Gneisenau* and *Prinz Eugen* to put to sea. S/Ldr Burton-Giles, the pilot of the first Hampden (AE202), brought his aircraft safely back to England after planting his *vegetables* in the allotted spot, but when he landed a wing tip had gone, an aileron had been damaged, the main-plane had been holed, an engine fairing had gone, one of the propellers had been hit, one rudder had been shot away, and one of the mainwheels punctured. Sgt. Hackney, the pilot of the second machine, found

*Ready for off. The pilot climbs aboard Hampden P1244 of 408 'Goose' Squadron, R.C.A.F., as a mechanic stands by with a trolley acc. to start the engines in 1942.*

'Mines were laid. . . .' Hampdens of 408 Squadron are prepared for a mine-laying mission in 1942. In the early part of the war 5 Group's Hampdens were alone responsible for Bomber Command's sea-mining campaign. 'Bomber' Harris commanded the Group for a time and it was he who first advocated this form of war against sea power (before the war) and eventually organised its introduction. ['Aeroplane'.

it impossible to lay his mine in the allotted position owing to insufficient cloud cover. The third Hampden, captained by W/Cdr S. T. Misselbrook, the C.O., failed to return.

In an earlier operation against the warships at Brest, in May 1941, a Hampden of 44 Squadron scored a direct hit on the *Gneisenau* with a heavy S.A.P. bomb.

Night-intruder operations were also among the duties of 5 Group's Hampdens during 1941 in addition to their main role of strategic bombing, and among the targets attacked on such occasions were searchlights and shipping. On the night of November 3 a Hampden (AE309) from 144 Squadron, North Luffenham, captained by F/Lt J. F. Craig, R.N.Z.A.F., scored a notable success whilst on an offensive patrol along the Frisian Islands. During a break in the snow and rain squalls which swept across the North Sea, Craig sighted a convoy of ten ships and made an accurate low-level attack on the largest vessel—a merchantman of some 10,000 tons—setting it on fire. It was learned afterwards that the German general

commanding the western anti-aircraft defences, Maj-Gen Felix Varda, was on board this ship and was among those killed as a result of the Hampden's attack. In April 1942, 144 Squadron transferred to Coastal Command as the first one of two Hampden units to be employed in the torpedo-bomber role. Four Hampden squadrons were eventually employed as torpedo-bombers but the story of these is outside the scope of this narrative.

Hampdens took part in the famous raid of March 3–4 1942 on the Renault works, near Paris—the first occasion when the principle of concentration of attack was genuinely employed—and a few months later shared in each of the three '1,000-bomber' raids. By then, though, their days as operational aircraft were numbered—5 Group being well on the way to becoming an all-Lancaster force—and on September 14–15 they flew on ops with Bomber Command for the last time, when aircraft of 408 'Goose' Squadron, R.C.A.F., from Balderton, bombed Wilhelmshaven.

## Specification

Hampden I: *Crew* 4; *power plant* two 980 h.p. Bristol Pegasus XVIII; *span* 69 ft. 2 in.; *length* 53 ft. 7 in.; *wing area* 668 sq. ft., *empty weight* 11,780 lb., *loaded weight* 18,756 lb.; *max. bomb load* 4,000 lb.; *max. speed* 265 m.p.h. at 15,500 ft.; *service ceiling* 22,700 ft.; *max. range* 1,990 miles with 2,000 lb. bomb load and 1,200 miles with max. bomb load; *armament* one fixed and one moveable .303 in. m.g. in nose and single or twin .303 in. m.g.s in dorsal and ventral positions.

P1166 'K-King' of 408 'Goose' Squadron, R.C.A.F., formates with a sister aircraft over England in 1942. ['Aeroplane'.

# Handley Page Halifax

Second of the R.A.F.'s new four-engine 'heavies' to enter service in World War II, the Halifax, was evolved from Air Ministry Specification P.13/36—the same Spec. that produced the unsuccessful Manchester (see Volume 1). To meet P.13/36, which called for an all-metal, mid-wing cantilever monoplane 'heavy medium' bomber, powered by two Rolls-Royce Vulture liquid-cooled engines, then still under development, Handley Page's chief designer, G. R. Volkert, and his team designed, in 1936–37, the H.P.56, a development of the unbuilt H.P.55 to B.1/35. Two prototypes were ordered in April 1937 but the following August, when the doubtful prospects of the Vulture had become apparent, the Air Ministry induced Handley Page, 'much against the company's wishes',* to take four Rolls-Royce Merlins instead.

The resulting aircraft, which was known initially as the H.P.57, was considerably larger and heavier than the original design—its wing span was nearly 100 ft. and its weight increased by almost 50 per cent—and the first prototype of two ordered exactly two years prior to the outbreak of war, L7244, made its initial flight on October 25 1939.

In accordance with the specification, the H.P.57 was designed to carry a number of 2,000-lb. bombs in racks under the fuselage floor. When, eventually, much larger bombs had to be carried, a special carrier had to be installed to carry them and distribute the load over the floor. This carrier took up vertical space in the bomb bay so that when these large bombs were carried the bomb doors were partially open, with resultant increased drag. At this stage of the war the Halifax was in full production, and to change and strengthen the floor to take directly the larger bombs would have caused too great a setback in production.

A pilot production order for 100 H.P.57s was placed in January 1939, and in 1940 it was decided to form an organisation known as the Halifax Group, to undertake really large-scale production. Besides the parent company—whose order for 100 Halifaxes was soon doubled—it comprised four main members, the first of which was the English Electric Company, which was already building Hampdens. Its first Halifax, a Mk. II, flew in August 1941. Other firms brought into the Halifax Group were: the London Aircraft Production Group (Chrysler Motors, Duple Bodies and Motors, Express Motor and Body Works, Park Royal

*Above: Halifax B.II Srs I W7676 'P-Peter' of 35 Squadron in flight over the Yorkshire countryside in May 1942. This machine is the subject of the five-view colour painting on pages 38 and 39. ['Aeroplane'.*

*Below: Another view of B.II Srs I 'P-Peter' W7676 of 35 Squadron taken later in 1942 when its fuselage roundels had been modified from Type A1 to Type C1 style. [Charles E. Brown.*

* The Design and Development of Weapons (H.M.S.O., 1964).

*B.II Srs I W1245 'B-Baker' of 78 Squadron circa late 1942.* [*I.W.M.*

Coachworks and the London Passenger Transport Board); Rootes Securities and Fairey Aviation. The latter two were not part of the organisation as originally planned but came in to replace de Havilland.

The second prototype Halifax, L7245, flew in August 1940 and was followed less than two months later by the first production aircraft, L9485. Unlike the original prototype both these aircraft had hydraulically operated Boulton Paul nose and tail turrets. L9485 flew 72 weeks after the issue of the first production drawings. Within another five weeks a Halifax squadron, No. 35, was being formed in Yorkshire by W/Cdr R. W. P. Collings. On the night of March 11–12 1941, just five months after the appearance of the production version, and when Handley Page had delivered nearly a score of Halifaxes to the R.A.F., 35 Squadron made its first operational sortie with the new aircraft. Six aircraft were sent to attack the dockyard at Le Havre but one of them, unable to see either the primary or the alternative target (Boulogne), bombed Dieppe instead. Another machine, failing to see the primary target even after repeated circuits and having insufficient fuel to proceed to the alternative target, was forced to jettison its bombs in the Channel. Tragedy

marred the mission, for one of the successful aircraft, while returning from Le Havre, was mistaken for an enemy aircraft on the return journey and shot down in flames at Normandy, Surrey, by one of our own night fighters. Only two members of the crew escaped by parachute and survived.

There was a disturbingly large number of hydraulic failures in the Halifax immediately following its entry into service. When it became obvious that hydraulic locks were not sufficient to ensure that the undercarriage remained retracted, particularly after damage, the hydraulic system was completely redesigned, much of the work being undertaken at 35 Squadron's base at Linton-on-Ouse. Tailwheels also gave trouble. These retracted forwards and were prone to stay retracted on landing, which often resulted in practically all 35 Squadron's ground personnel crawling under the fuselage and lifting the aircraft bodily while sandbags were stacked, since jacks were not yet available. Very soon retractable tailwheels were abandoned.

Not until July 1941 was the existence of the Halifax

officially disclosed to the British public at large. The announcement followed a daylight attack on the notorious German battle-cruiser *Scharnhorst*, which had slipped out of Brest. Fifteen Halifaxes from 35 and 76 Squadrons were despatched and fourteen of them reached the target, where they were met by what appeared to be between twelve and eighteen Bf.109s. Every one of these fourteen Halifaxes was hit by fire from the fighters or by flak. Five failed to return and five more were badly damaged. Nevertheless the bombers scored five direct hits on the *Scharnhorst* and forced her to put back for Brest with 3,000 tons of flood water inside her. The *Scharnhorst* remained in Brest until an escape with the *Gneisenau* enabled them both to regain their home ports, albeit in a very battered condition.

The Halifax was withdrawn from daylight operations after a final raid on the two battle-cruisers at Brest in December 1941 because increasing fighter opposition threatened to make the casualty rate in such raids prohibitive.

As the number of Halifax squadrons grew, the Mk. I was supplanted by the Mk. II, which had various combinations of turrets and guns and sacrificed speed for fire power or vice versa.

Third squadron to fly Halifaxes was No. 10, which first used the type operationally on the second of the two daylight raids on Brest in which Halifaxes figured in December 1942. W/Cdr D. C. T. Bennett was appointed C.O. of the squadron in mid-April 1942, and at the end of the month some of the Halifaxes,

*Pilot's cockpit of a Halifax B.II photographed in August 1942. Dual controls were not normally fitted.* [*I.W.M.*

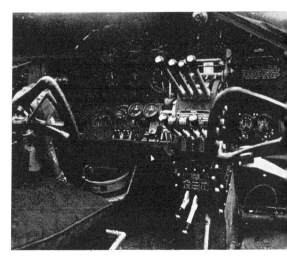

with others from 76 Squadron and Lancasters from 44 Squadron—all of them operating from advanced airfields in Scotland—made two attacks with *Johnnie Walker* mines on the pocket-battleship *Tirpitz*, at anchor in the Aasfjord, Norway. Each Halifax carried five of the 1,000-lb. spherical mines—their bomb doors wouldn't close properly as a result although this was of no great importance—and the idea was to drop them so they rolled down on the shore side of the *Tirpitz*, which lay only 50 feet from the steep sloping banks of the Aasfjord. The mines were fitted with appropriate depth fuses and it was hoped that they would get under the comparatively vulnerable bottom of the hull and blow it in. Both raids proved unsuccessful, and in the first one, W/Cdr Bennett's Halifax II W1041 'B-Beer' was shot down in Norway; however, Bennett and three other members of his crew escaped and eventually returned to England, Bennett being chosen in August 1942 to command the newly formed Pathfinder Force, which was later given group status (8 Group). Incidentally, the original Halifax squadron, No. 35, was one of the five units chosen to form the nucleus of the Pathfinder Force. In 1943 the first Canadian Halifax unit, 405 'Vancouver' Squadron, also joined the P.F.F.

When the P.F.F. began to operate, a vast improvement was affected in the technique of night bombing,

and from early 1943 the Halifaxes played a prominent part in the mounting round-the-clock offensive which 'Bomber' Harris had promised would 'scourge the Third Reich from end to end'.

In the Battle of Hamburg, which began in July, the revolutionary 'magic eye' radar navigational aid known as H2S made its operation début, Halifaxes of 35 Squadron being among the small force that actually introduced it. (A Halifax, albeit not a squadron machine, was the first aircraft ever to be fitted with H2S. Initial trials were made in V9977, a Mk. II, on March 27 1942, but tragically the machine crashed in South Wales on June 7 that year, killing the entire crew and five scientists who were on board. Almost half the H2S research team was wiped out.)

By now the Halifax B.II Series IA was coming into service. This version retained the standard four-gun Boulton Paul rear turret, but in the dorsal position was a compact Boulton Paul 'Defiant'-type turret, mounting four guns instead of the earlier—and bulbous—'Hudson'-type turret's two. It also had a neat, moulded Perspex nose mounting a single hand-operated .303 in. Vickers K gas-operated gun. Powered by Merlin XXs or XXIIs, this cleaned-up model had an edge of about 20 m.p.h. in cruising speed over the earlier versions. An interim version of the Halifax II was the Mk. II Srs. I (Special), and eventually this also

had a 'Defiant'-type mid-upper turret. To overcome a shortage of Messier undercarriages, the Halifax V, using a Dowty undercarriage, was introduced in 1943, and the two main versions of this, the Mk. V Srs. I (Special) and Srs. IA, corresponded to the Mk. II variants. Some Mk. II Srs. IAs and 'V Srs. IAs were fitted with H2S or, alternatively, a ventral gun position mounting a single .50 in. Browning gun.

Several Merlin-powered Halifaxes were involved in unexplained crashes in which the aircraft got into a vertical dive. The cause was eventually traced to rudder stalling: the triangular fin stalled under certain conditions, and turbulent air passing the gap between fin and rudder, locked the latter hard over. The trouble was cured by fitting the large rectangular fin that became part of the Halifax recognition 'trademark'.

Talking of the Halifax's tail brings to mind the incident involving 10 Squadron's Halifax DT792 'O-Oboe'—believed to be a Mk. II Series I (Special)—during the third in the famous series of four fire raids on Hamburg in the summer of 1943. Before reaching the target the Hally was attacked by a Ju 88 night fighter, and the pilot, F/O J. G. Jenkins, was compelled to jettison his bombs and take evasive action. The rear gunner eventually shot the Ju down in flames but not before both of the Hally's elevators had been shot away,

*Bomb-aimer at his station in a Halifax B.II. [I.W.M.*

*Flight engineer at his station in a Halifax B.II. [I.W.M.*

*View aft inside the rear fuselage of a Merlin-engined Halifax of 419 'Moose' Squadron, R.C.A.F., showing the ammunition rails (upper right) running down to the tail turret.*

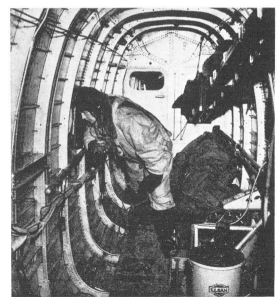

the wings and fuselage damaged and the port tyre punctured. Miraculously none of the crew was injured and Jenkins, despite the difficulty of controlling his aircraft, returned to base and made a safe landing, Jovially named 'Bring-'em-back-alive Jenkins' because of his not infrequent habit—due to circumstances entirely beyond his control—of being unable to release his bombs or mines, this same pilot (by now a Flight Lieutenant) was unlucky enough to find himself in a very uncomfortable position once again on September 22–23, while engaged in a sortie against Hanover in Halifax II Series IA HR924 'N-Nuts'. This time an attacking enemy fighter shot away his windscreen and extensively damaged both sides of the fuselage and also the hydraulic system. Although every effort was made to release the bombs during the return journey they stubbornly refused to leave the racks, and on reaching England Jenkins and his crew were ordered to head the aircraft out to sea again and bale out—which they all did successfully.

By the end of 1943 the Yorkshire-based No. 4 Bomber Group was entirely equipped with Halifaxes and it operated the type throughout the remainder of the European war. At the time of its peak strength

(March 1945) the group had 13 Halifax Squadrons.

The R.C.A.F. Bomber Group—6 Group—which formed in Yorkshire in late 1942, also adopted the Halifax. This was not its only aircraft, but each of its ultimate total of 14 squadrons was for a time solely equipped with the Halifax. Whereas 4 Group's squadrons were based in an area to the east and south of York, the Canadian Group's lay in an area to the north and west of the ancient cathedral city.

Although the Merlin-engined Halifax did valuable work with Bomber Command, its all-round performance was always unsatisfactory because it was underpowered. Labouring along at only moderate heights it was easy meat for enemy fighters, and by 1943 losses had become serious. The type continued to be unsatisfactory throughout 1943 and, to quote the Official History of the strategic bombing offensive, 'it was not until about February 1944, when the Mark III

*B.II Srs I (Special) BB324 'X-X-Ray' of 10 Squadron sporting on its nose a bulldog in a sailor's hat and the legend* Wings for Victory, *photographed in April 1943. This particular Hally was eventually lost in a raid on Mulheim on June 22–23 1943.* ['Aeroplane'].

became available in quantity, that the Halifax began to hold its own against the formidable defences of the Third Reich'. Even then it still had its shortcomings— notably in range and bomb load—and never anything like so potent a weapon as its contemporary, the Lancaster.

The decision to introduce the Halifax III (which had the Handley Page Type Number H.P.61) followed tests begun in 1943 with the Handley Page's 'hack' Mk. II R9534 re-engined with 1,615 h.p. Bristol Hercules VIs. Production models had Hercules XVIs and the extra power which these afforded boosted the Halifax's performance and permitted a maximum all-up weight of 65,000 lb. The 'first off', HX226, flew in July 1943, and during the type's production run the wing span was increased from 98 ft. 10 in. to 104 ft. 2 in. The increase in wing area improved the operational ceiling, and extended, curved wing-tips became standard on all subsequent marks. No. 2 fuel tank was transferred from the intermediate section to the centre section of the wings and provision made for additional (optional) fuel tanks in the starboard outer bomb cells in the centre section. Other features included a retractable tailwheel (previously introduced

on the Mk. I but abandoned as related earlier) and an H2S scanner or ventral gun position (one .50 in. Browning) as standard.

First squadrons to receive the Halifax B.III were Nos. 433 (R.C.A.F.) and 466 (R.A.A.F.); this was in November 1943, and by the end of the year several squadrons of both 4 and 6 Groups were using the type. Bomber Command's Merlin-engined Halifaxes were completely supplanted by the new version during the next few months, the last squadrons to operate Merlin Hallies being Nos. 346 and 347 (Free French Air Force) Squadrons at Elvington, in 4 Group, who changed over to Mk. IIIs in June and July 1944, respectively, soon after they had formed.

In the months immediately preceding D-Day, Halifaxes played a full part in the so-called 'Transportation Plan'—the offensive against the enemy's rail communications system in France and Belgium. Following the invasion of Europe, the bombers returned to their early role of daylight bombers—but now as a semi-tactical force, their objectives being gun emplacements on the French coast, strong points and troop concentrations, all of which were attacked with uncanny accuracy.

In addition to operating in close support of our forces and disorganising the enemy's communications, the Hallies waged a vigorous offensive against V-weapons. The high-water mark was reached in August 1944 when 4 Group alone flew 3,629 sorties. By this time the *Luftwaffe* was, generally speaking, too enfeebled to offer very serious resistance although as recently as June the group created a Bomber Command record by destroying 33 fighters.

4 Group also undertook emergency transport work and in little over one week ferried nearly half a million gallons of petrol to an airfield near Brussels to meet the urgent needs of the British Second Army during the heroic struggle at Arnhem.

Oil targets now returned to the priority list and of special significance was an attack on the oil plant at Homberg in the Ruhr on August 27. A force of 216 Halifax IIIs from 4 Group and 27 Mosquitoes and Lancasters from 8 Group was despatched, with an escort of an almost equal number of Spitfires of Fighter Command. Only one enemy fighter—a Bf.110—was seen by the bomber crews and it was driven off by the Spitfires before it could do any damage. Heavy anti-aircraft fire was encountered in

the target area but none of the bombers was brought down and all the aircraft subsequently returned safely home. This was the first major daylight operation by Bomber Command against a German target in 1944 and the first also in which Bomber Command had ever penetrated beyond the Rhine with fighter cover. The target was partly obscured by cloud and although the damage done to it was somewhat scattered it was, in places, quite severe.

Some idea of the size of the Halifax's contribution to the war effort during 1944 can be gained from the activities of 4 Group (the only all-Halifax group) alone. It flew 25,464 sorties (on all types of operation including bombing, sea-mining and emergency transport) at a cost of 402 aircraft missing.

Smashing attacks on Hanover, Magdeburg and Stuttgart came at the beginning of 1945. Cologne, Munster, Osnabrück and many other 'old favourites' of Bomber Command also came under the bombsights once more. The Halifaxes of 4 and 6 Groups attacked them by day and by night until the time came to pound the great railway centres preparatory to the climax of the war on the ground, the crossing of the Rhine.

In March, 4 Group dropped its record weight of bombs on Germany in a series of outstandingly successful raids. The loss rate for this month was to be the lowest in the Command.

Two new marks of Halifax were in service alongside the B.III in the closing months of the European war—the B. Mks. VI and VII. Both had a pressure-transfer fuel system, with 'grouped tanks' (one group per engine), additional tankage, special carburettor filters over the carburettor intakes and HS2 as a standard fitment. More and more attention was being paid to preparations for a final campaign in the Far East, and 'tropicalisation' was the order of the day for new types. The B.VI had four 1,675 h.p. Hercules 100 engines which gave it a maximum speed of 312 m.p.h. at 22,000 ft., and improved its all round performance. It had an all-up weight of 68,000 lb. and the first example, NP715, first flew on October 10 1944. The B.VI served in 76, 77, 78, 102, 158, 346, 347 and 640 Squadrons of 4 Group but was only just becoming

established when hostilities in Europe ended. The B.VII had Hercules XVI engines—the power-plant of the B.III. This mark came into being because airframe production exceeded supply of Hercules 100 engines. It was used primarily by the squadrons of 62 'Beaver' Base and its sub-stations in 6 (R.C.A.F.) Group, i.e. 408, 426, 432 and (to a small extent) 415 Squadrons.

The last occasion when Halifaxes of Bomber Command operated in force against the enemy was on April 25 1945, when a heavy daylight attack was made

on coastal gun batteries on Wangerooge Island in the East Frisians. On May 2–3 1945, Halifaxes of 100 (Bomber Support) Group flew diversionary R.C.M. (sometimes with bomb-dropping) sorties against Flensburg, Schleswig-Holstein and elsewhere, in support of a Main Force attack on Kiel—Bomber Command's last raid of the war.

Halifaxes of Bomber Command flew more than 82,000 operational sorties during the war, and dropped nearly a quarter of a million tons of bombs. One

*B.II Series IA JN894 stands beside a wrecked Ju 88 on an airfield in Italy circa early 1944—probably Celone, base of 462 (later 614) Squadron. The H2S blister has been removed from the photograph by the wartime censor.* [*I.W.M.*

thousand eight hundred and thirty-three Halifaxes were reported missing.

With 100 Group of Bomber Command Halifaxes waged a fantastic war of their own—a war of the ether, jamming and confusing the enemy's radio and utterly confounding his fighter controllers. Other Halifaxes, operating with 'Special Duties' squadrons of Bomber Command, dropped secret agents in enemy-held territory and countless loads of arms and supplies to resistance movements.

At the end of the European war, Bomber Command's Halifax squadrons were either disbanded, transferred to Transport Command and soon re-equipped with Dakotas, Yorks or Liberators, or else—in the case of some units of 6 Group—rearmed with Lancasters before returning to Canada. Nearly all the surviving Halifaxes of 4 and 6 Groups found their way to Rawcliffe, York, or 29 Maintenance Unit, High Ercall, Shropshire, and by 1947 most of them had been scrapped. Today just about the sole remains are a series of nose panels featuring colourful unofficial insignia salvaged from several 6 Group aircraft at the above-mentioned 'graveyards' and now displayed in the R.C.A.F.'s fine Museum at Rockcliffe, Ottawa.

In the middle of 1942 Halifax B.IIs and crews of 10 and 76 Squadrons were posted to Aqir in Palestine (the squadrons in the U.K. subsequently being reformed) and joined by other non-operational squadrons which acted as ground servicing units. Attacks were made on Tobruk and Benghazi from advanced landing grounds in Egypt and in September the units combined to form 462 (R.A.A.F.) Squadron. Thereafter the squadron's operational area was steadily widened to include much of North Africa, Italy, Greece, Crete, the Dodecanese Islands and Sicily. Early in 1944 it dropped leaflets on Greece, Crete, Rhodes, Leros and Samos, and in March, shortly after having moved to Italy, it was renumbered 614 Squadron and given a pathfinder role (a new 462 Halifax Squadron later formed in England). 614 Squadron continued to fly Halifax B.IIs of various sub-types until early 1945, when it was completely re-armed with Liberator B.VIIIs, which latter type it had already been using since August 1944. Another bomber unit which flew Halifaxes in the Middle East

*. . . And one that didn't. Wreckage of JB921 'M-Mother'* **of** *78 Squadron which crashed in Holland on the night of* **May** *13–14 1943* [*via G. Zwanenburg.*

*A 2,000-lb. H.C. bomb and small bomb containers holding incendiaries arrives at Halifax II Srs IA 'G-George's' dispersal at an R.C.A.F. bomber station 'somewhere in England' in 1943 or early 1944.*

was 178 Squadron, which used Mk. IIs from May to September 1943.

After V.E. Day a few Halifax B.VIs were sent from Britain to the Far East to harass the Japanese, but these aircraft were not used for bombing; they were employed in a radio-countermeasures role and their activities do not come within the scope of the present work.

Countless stirring tales of the exploits of Halifaxes and their crews are to be found in the official archives and elsewhere—tales like this one concerning a machine detailed to bomb a target in Hanover: As it neared its objective it was hit by heavy flak and part of the fuselage was pushed in and a hole torn in its side near the navigator's compartment. The aircraft shuddered and began to vibrate so violently that the instruments could not be read. Then an engine fell out. Damage prevented the jettisoning of the bombs, so the pilot, with all navigational aids u/s, turned for home. An icy blast beat upon the crew from the huge hole ripped in the fuselage. After desperate and unsuccessful attempts to free the bombs the largest of them was released with the bay still closed; to everyone's relief it took the broken bomb doors with it. As the English coast was neared, the crew was still struggling feverishly to get rid of the rest of the load and the pilot had to fly out to sea again until the last bomb had been dropped. The Halifax could not be abandoned as the wireless operator's parachute had been torn open. With fuel running dangerously low they reached an emergency airfield. The pilot, having tested the damaged undercarriage by bumping it on the runway, did another circuit and landing. This time the leg collapsed but the crew emerged unhurt from the ensuing crash. Before the Hally came to rest, a second engine had fallen from it.

On another occasion the crew of a burning Halifax, which had been hit and set alight just after dropping its bombs on Essen, made an amazing flight of 150 miles across enemy-held territory before baling out behind the Allied lines. When the bomber was hit, cushions on the rest position between the wing spars caught fire and, although the crew used extinguishers and even coffee from six vacuum flasks, the fire would

*A 6 Group Halifax is made ready to deliver a load of 500-pounders to the enemy in 1944 or '45. The gas cylinders beneath the fuselage contained nitrogen which was used to 'top-up' the wing fuel tanks and thus minimise the risk of fire in the event of their being holed by flak or fighters.*

not go out. The draught from the open bomb doors fanned the flames and soon the fabric on the fuselage floor, and the wooden supports of the rest position were ablaze. Part of the oxygen system exploded and the rubber oxygen tubes caught fire. The insulation round the aircraft's heating system also caught fire. In this inferno of flame and dense acrid smoke, the intercom failed. The fire reached within an inch or two of the main fuel-balance line running along the rear spar. It was then impossible to transfer petrol from the starboard wing tanks because the wires to the cock had become red hot. With the cockpit so full of smoke that he could not see his instruments, the pilot flew with the main bomber stream until he crossed the fighting lines. By this time the electrical system had burned away and all navigational aids had been destroyed. When orders came to abandon the aircraft, the wireless operator had to be helped out because his parachute had opened inside the fuselage; he held the canopy in his arms while two of his comrades threw him out.

A somewhat different kind of fire story was that told by a veteran R.C.A.F. crew of 35 (Pathfinder) Squadron who brought their badly crippled Halifax back from the Baltic port of Stettin after being accidentally bombed with incendiaries by one of our own aircraft on the night of April 20–21 1943. Two incendiaries struck the aircraft. One exploded in the flight engineer's compartment and that set the bomber on fire. The second incendiary was found after landing at base. It was inside one of the wing fuel tanks, but by some miraculous good fortune it had not exploded. 'We'd just dropped our bombs', said the captain, P/O W. S. 'Rocky' Sherk, 'and were turning off the target when there was a hell of an explosion in the kite. We thought at first it was a direct flak hit. Something hit right behind my seat and kept on going to explode in the engineer's compartment below [*sic*]. Luckily he'd just come up to stand beside me about 30 seconds before it happened. Most of the instruments were blown up and my uniform was on fire.' The aircraft went into a spiral dive. The controls were all u/s and the fire was burning away inside, so Sherk gave orders to bale out. They lost about 5,000 feet, and then the pilot found he could steer after a fashion by gunning and throttling back the engines on alternative sides. While Sherk steered a very rough course for the coast, another member of the crew, 'Scrammy' McGladrey, was beating out the flames, and the engineer, Sgt Doug. Bebensee, was feverishly trying to get some of the controls working again. He finally managed to get

*B.VII 'Y-Yoke' of 408 'Goose' Squadron, R.C.A.F., takes off from its base at Linton-on-Ouse in the closing months of the war.*

some of them in order, ailerons with no rudder. Two of the crew baled out. F/Lt 'Moe' Morison, the navigator, on being ordered to jump, jettisoned the escape hatch, hitched on his parachute and then took a look down below. 'There was a lovely mess of fires and light flak', he said, 'and I thought that this wasn't a very healthy place to jump into, so I decided to wait a bit.' McGladrey had thrown his 'chute at the fire trying to put out the blaze, so he yelled to Morison to wait for him because he'd decided to hitch-hike down on Morison's 'chute. While he was trying to fasten himself to his comrade's 'chute, Sherk got the Halifax under partial control so they decided to stay aboard. Morison's maps of that part of the country had blown out through the escape hatch, so he pin-pointed the way to the coast. There were some other maps which he used later. F/O McGladrey commented afterwards that he would like to start a fire-fighter's club. 'I grabbed the ruddy hand extinguisher', he said, 'and the blasted thing wouldn't work. It sounds crazy now, but I can remember stopping right there and then, taking out my flashlight and reading the instructions on the side of the extinguisher to see if I was doing it right. Finally I threw it away. The bomb has split open the back of the skipper's seat, and the stuffing was flaming away. I grabbed the burning material in handfuls and tossed it out of the kite. I had gloves on so I didn't get burned.'

After having bombed Saarbrücken on January 13–14 1945, Halifax III MZ465 'Y-Yorker' of 51

Squadron had nine feet of its nose sliced off by the tail of another bomber which crossed its path; but it struggled back to England, with only three of its instruments still working, to make a perfect landing. Some of the skin on the nose was bent round and gave some protection against the wind which whistled through the aircraft as it flew home at 7,000 feet. But the captain, F/O A. L. Wilson, and his remaining crew, were frozen as they struggled to keep the Hally flying. (The navigator and the bomb-aimer, neither of whom were then wearing parachutes, had fallen out of the bomber at the time of the collision.) The four engines continued to function perfectly after the collision, although the propellers were dented, probably by bits of wreckage which shook loose and flew off the fuselage. The radio was still working five minutes after the collision, but had to be shut off because of shorting; blue sparks were playing around the aircraft and there was danger of fire. In that short five minutes, before the radio was cut off, the operator was able to send out an S.O.S. which was received in England. As a result 'Y-Yorker' was given special landing aids when it landed on an emergency airfield. The intercom was u/s as well as the A.S.I., the D.R. compass, and many other vital instruments for flying and navigation. 'Y-Yorker' dived 1,500 feet after the collision, with the pilot struggling to gain control. He

managed to do this and brought the machine up to 11,000 feet again. At this height it stalled, but he managed to keep it at 7,000 feet and at this height flew home.

'Y-Yorker's' squadron operated from Snaith in Yorkshire. A near neighbour was 578 Squadron based at Burn, just outside Selby, and on March 30–31 1944 the gallantry and devotion to duty of P/O Cyril Joe Barton of 578 Squadron earned him a posthumous V.C., the only such award to be won by a Halifax crew-member. His aircraft, B.III LK797 'E-Easy'—named *Excalibur* and sporting an emblem depicting a hand emerging from the base of a cloud and grasping the sword of the legendary King Arthur—was badly damaged by enemy fighters, while *en route* to Nuremburg, its target. One of the Halifax's engines was damaged, its guns put out of action so that the gunners were unable to return the enemy's fire, and the intercom rendered u/s. In the confusion which followed the failure of the intercom a signal was misinterpreted and the navigator, bomb-aimer and wireless operator baled out. Despite the obvious dangers, Barton was determined to finish the job he had come to do and so he pressed on to the target and released the bombs himself. As he turned for home the propeller of the damaged engine flew off. Two fuel tanks were leaking but all this did not deter Barton who, without navigational aids and in spite of strong headwinds, successfully avoided the most heavily defended areas on his route. Eventually he crossed the English coast only

Handley Page Halifax B. Mk. III NR152
of No. 466 (B) Squadron, based at Driffield,
Yorks., from June 1944 to May 1945.

*The remaining views will be found overleaf.*

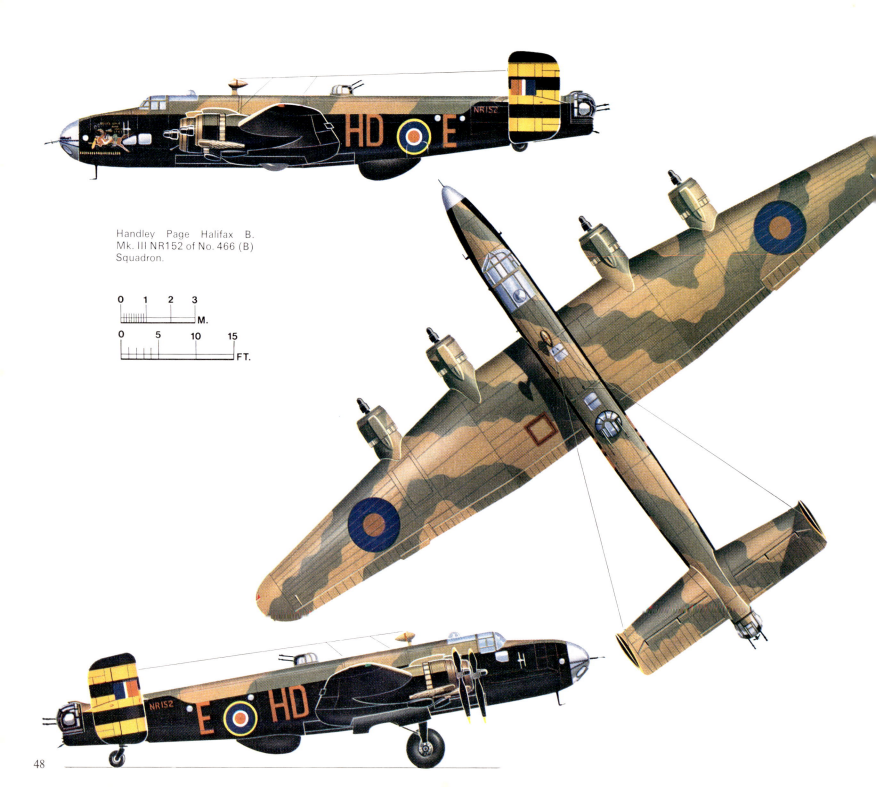

Handley Page Halifax B.
Mk. III NR152 of No. 466 (B)
Squadron.

48

00 miles north of his base. By now the fuel supply was nearly exhausted, and before a suitable landing place could be found one of the port engines stopped. The Halifax was too low to be abandoned successfully so Barton ordered the three remaining members of his crew to take up their crash stations. Then, with only one engine working, he made a gallant attempt to land clear of houses over which he was flying. The aircraft finally crashed on a slag heap and Barton lost his life. His three comrades survived.

Perhaps the most terrifying experience of any Halifax crew-member was that of Sgt A. L. Morrison, Canadian bomb-aimer of Halifax III MZ422 'N-Nuts' of 427 Lion Squadron, R.C.A.F., on the occasion of a raid on Chemnitz, on February 14–15 1945. 'N-Nuts', captained by F/O V. S. Roy, was suddenly attacked by a night fighter on the homeward flight. Fire immediately broke out in the centre fuselage and port wing. Roy ordered his crew to bale out but before they could do so the German fighter attacked again and the Hally blew up. The navigator and the flight engineer were thrown clear and parachuted to earth. The bomb-aimer however, fell 10,000 feet, clinging to a section of the bomber's nose and without a parachute. By an amazing stroke of luck he landed in some fir trees, which broke his fall, and tumbled into the snow. His German captors gave him a certificate to prove that his remarkable experience was true.

A total of 6,176 Halifaxes were built before production ended in 1946, although, of course, they were not all bombers. Four Bomber Command Halifax

*Halifax B.III LW380 'PT-B' The Bird of Prey of 420 'Snowy Owl' Squadron, R.C.A.F., at Tholthorpe during the closing months of the war.*

B.IIIs are known to have passed the century mark on wartime operations and these—all of which survived the war (only to be scrapped afterwards)—were LV907 *Friday the Thirteenth* of 158 Squadron (128 sorties), LV937 of 578 and 51 Squadrons (at least 100 sorties), LW587 of 578 Squadron (at least 104 sorties) and MZ527, also of 578 Squadron (at least 105 sorties). The last two aircraft flew their 100th ops. simultaneously— on March 3–4 1945, against Kamen. Another Halifax III, LV917 *Clueless* of 158 Squadron, is known to have flown 99 operations and seems to have had an extra one 'chalked up' on its nose for luck.

*This Halifax III, MZ465, 'MH-Y' of 51 Squadron, had its nose chopped clean off in a mid-air collision with another Halifax over Germany on February 13–14 1945, yet returned safely to England (see story on opposite page).*

## Specification

Halifax B.I Srs I (B.III data in parentheses where different): *Crew* 7; *power plant* four 1,280 h.p. Rolls-Royce Merlin X (1,615 h.p. Bristol Hercules XVI); *span* 98 ft. 10 in. (late series B.IIIs 104 ft. 2 in.); *length* 70 ft. 1 in. (71 ft. 7 in.); *wing area* 1,250 sq. ft. (late srs B.IIIs 1,275 sq. ft.); *empty weight* 33,860 lb. (37,240 lb.) *max. t.o. weight* 55,000 lb. (65,000 lb); *max. bomb load* 13,000 lb.; *max. speed* 262 m.p.h. at 17,750 ft. (281 m.p.h. at 13,500 ft.); *service ceiling* at max. weight 22,800 ft. (20,000 ft.); *range* 1,000 miles with max. bomb load (1,077 miles with max. bomb load); *armament* twin .303 in. m.g. in nose turret, and four .303 in. m.g. in tail turret, single .303 in. m.g. in beam positions optional (one .303 in. m.g. in nose, and four .303 in. m.g. in dorsal and tail turrets; some a/c also had one .50 in. gun in ventral position instead of H2S scanner).

# Lockheed Vega Ventura

Late in 1939 Lockheed proposed to the British Purchasing Commission, which was already well pleased with the Hudson medium reconnaissance bomber which it had ordered for R.A.F. Coastal Command, an improved aerial weapon, the Model 37, developed from the Model 18 Lodestar civil transport. In February 1940 the British Purchasing Commission placed an initial order for 25 and Lockheed promptly subcontracted the business to its subsidiary, Vega, to be manufactured in its new factory at Burbank, California. The new bomber was named the Ventura and the first example (AE658) flew on July 31 1941. It resembled the Hudson in overall appearance but was heavier and more powerful, and has its dorsal gun turret mounted further forward to allow a wider field of fire. Also, the underside of the fuselage incorporated a ventral gun position which gave it a distinctive kink.

Pleased with flight test data, Britain ordered a further 650 Venturas, but many were retained by the U.S. Army and Navy so that only 394 were actually delivered to the R.A.F. It was decided to employ the Ventura as a day bomber with 2 Group, Bomber Command, and the type first entered service with 21 Squadron at Bodney, Norfolk, in the early summer of 1942. This unit had previously flown Blenheim IVs, latterly from Malta, and after having re-formed in England and practised with some 'new' Blenheim IVs it received its first two Venturas on May 31. The build-up to operational strength and readiness was slow but by the end of November the squadron had

*21 Squadron's Ventura II AE839 'A-Apple' warms up its engines at Methwold on January 12 1943. Because of its porcine fuselage the Ventura was dubbed the 'Flying Pig' or just 'Pig'. [Charles E. Brown.*

21 Ventura Is and IIs on charge and was re-located at Methwold, from which base it was soon to begin operations. It finally went into action on November 3: the target was Hengelo in Holland and three Venturas were despatched; one bombed the primary target and blew up the northern railway track, another bombed the railway between Apeldoorn and Amersfoort, while the third—the leader—was forced to return early and make a crash-landing in England.

A series of small-scale attacks, each employing only two Venturas, followed this operation in quick succession, and again the objectives were in Holland.

Meanwhile two further Ventura squadrons had formed—Nos. 464 (R.A.A.F.) and 487 (R.N.Z.A.F.). Both units were based at Feltwell, and from November 9, in conjunction with 21 Squadron, which temporarily stood down from operations, they concentrated on

low-level formation practice. The Ventura wing was fully trained by the end of November and it then stood by for a week awaiting suitable weather for a low-level daylight attack on the Philips radio and valve factory at Eindhoven in Holland, which was thought to be responsible for about one-third of Germany's supply of radio components. The raid—which was code-named Operation *Oyster*—was finally mounted on December 6. Forty-seven Venturas were included in the force despatched, the rest consisting of 36 Bostons and ten Mosquitoes. The Venturas formed the third wave and were detailed to go in at 200 ft. or less with bombs and machine-gun fire; each one carried a mixed load of two 1-hour or $\frac{1}{2}$-hour delayed 250-lb. high-explosive bombs and forty 30-lb. incendiaries. The bombers flew out at 'zero feet' and the Ventura section,

with 464 Squadron leading, met considerable opposition from enemy flak, losing one aircraft shot down by a light coastal battery and another soon afterwards as the formation swept across a well-defended airfield. Two aircraft of 464 Squadron were severely damaged before reaching Eindoven, but although one, with five feet of its wing shot away, was forced to retire, the other continued its task with a damaged port engine.

The Ventura force arrived over its objective, the southern group of factory buildings, at 12.40 p.m., and although it was obscured by smoke from an attack made six minutes previously by Bostons, almost every aircraft scored hits. Several Venturas were shot down or else probably crashed into unseen buildings at this stage—they were all attacking from roof-top

height—and the survivors had to fight their way back damaged either by gunfire or by seagulls and ducks encountered in flight. Total Ventura losses on this raid were nine aircraft—including one flown by W/Cdr F. C. Seavill, C.O. of 487 Squadron, which had crashed in flames on the airfield on the Dutch coast—with a further 37 damaged; thus only one machine returned completely intact. There were some narrow escapes. S/Ldr L. H. Trent, a New Zealander in the R.A.F., saw an aircraft only ten yards away to starboard blown to pieces. Another 487 Squadron Ventura was hit by flak which ignited some Very cartridges, filling the bomber with smoke before they were finally extinguished. Two more New Zealand Venturas flew so close to one another at one stage that their wings actually touched, 'with a tearing sound', but, as both were flying at the same speed, no damage was caused. Several crews did have their machines damaged, however, when they struck trees while trying to get away at low level after bombing.

After this spectacular raid the main commitments of the three Ventura squadrons were *Circus* and *Ramrod* operations—but always flown at high level now. Occasional air–sea rescue searches were flown, and in addition to a strenuous training programme the wing, during the first fortnight of March, co-operated with the Army in large-scale manœuvres in southern England (Exercise *Spartan*). Mock bombing attacks were made on road and rail centres and towns, umpires deciding which machines had been 'shot down' by flak or fighters and what effect the 'bombing' had had on the 'enemy'.

Targets attacked in the *Circus* operations included steelworks, airfields, dockyards, and railway marshalling yards in the coastal areas of northern France, Belgium and Holland, and it was the normal practice of each squadron to provide 12 Venturas, in two standard 'boxes' of six, on each occasion. The bombers would cross the Channel at low level to avoid detection by enemy radar and then climb quickly to their bombing height of 10,000 ft., swiftly diving again to sea-level after the attack and leaving their escort to handle any pursuing enemy fighters. The Venturas met plenty of opposition, both from flak and fighters on these tip-and-run raids, but actual losses were light. Very often at this time crews reached their targets only to find them obscured by cloud, so that they were compelled to return without bombing. Time and again

*Formation of 21 Squadron Venturas from Methwold on January 12 1943, with Mk. II AE856 'Z-Zebra', subject of the five-view colour painting on pages 52 and 53, nearest the camera. ['Aeroplane'.*

*Close-up of 'Z-Zebra's' Donald Duck insignia. [Charles E. Brown.*

crews stood by for operations, only to find that missions were cancelled at the last minute owing to low cloud being reported in the target area.

Despite its apparent ability to sustain severe battle damage and yet remain in the air, the Ventura was a disappointment as a day bomber, being slow, heavy, unmanœuvrable and lacking in good defensive armament. Insofar as 464 and 487 Squadrons were concerned, a further handicap was the fact that Feltwell airfield turned into a sea of mud after heavy rain, and great relief was felt when those units moved, early in April, to Methwold. (21 Squadron simultaneously transferring from that station to Oulton.) Specific targets attacked by the Venturas that month included the marshalling yards at Caen, Haarlem, Abbeville and Outreau (near Boulogne), and shipping at Cherbourg and Dieppe. In the Outreau raid intense flak forced crews to drop their bombs on an adjoining

*A Ventura of 21 Squadron banks steeply for the camera on January 12 1943. ['Aeroplane'.*

steelworks. Several aircraft were badly hit, and Sgt G. T. Whitwell, R.N.Z.A.F. pilot of a 487 Squadron Ventura flying with a crew of three Englishmen, had his left arm shattered by shrapnel during his run-in. He was in great pain but with his good arm he carried on until his bomb-aimer reported 'bombs gone', and only then turned for home, where, despite his disability, he landed his machine with an engine on fire at the strange and very small airfield at Lympne. He received an immediate D.F.M.—487 Squadron's first decoration. The flak that day was the worst the New Zealand squadron had encountered in its 20 raids but miraculously no aircraft were shot down. All were damaged,

though, and in one no less than 134 holes were counted.

Shortly after this incident came the blackest day in 487 Squadron's entire history—May 3, when a disastrous mission was flown against Amsterdam. Eleven crews were briefed and they were told that they were to bomb the power-station in the Dutch capital and, at the same time, create a diversion for another raid by Bostons a few minutes later on the power-stations at Ijmuiden; the main object of the attacks was to assist the Dutch Resistance Movement and

*Joybelle, a Ventura of 487 Squadron, R.N.Z.A.F., receives its quota of 250- and 500-pounders at Methwold in May 1943.*

encourage Dutch workers in strikes then being organised in defiance of the Germans. No. 487's crews were warned that their target was well defended but were urged to press home the attack regardless of opposition.

The Venturas, flying in two formations, were led by S/Ldr L. H. Trent, with a young Englishman, F/Lt A. V. Duffill, as his deputy. The bombers left Methwold in the late afternoon, rendezvoused with their close escort of six Spitfire squadrons over Coltishall, nearer the coast, and then flew over the sea. As they skimmed over the water the crews tested all the guns and fused the bombs, unaware that the plan that

*Ventura II AE854 of 487 Squadron, R.N.Z.A.F., in flight in May 1943.*

had been outlined to them only a few hours earlier had already misfired.

That very afternoon the German governor of Holland was paying a state visit to Haarlem, which was about mid-way between the Dutch coast and the bombers' objective, and to protect the area during his visit fighter reinforcements had been brought from as far afield as Norway and France. An even more serious misfortune was the fact that a fighter diversionary wing had made a serious mistake and got twenty minutes ahead of schedule. Before they were recalled they broke through the German radar screen, and enemy fighters were thus given time to assemble in strength ready to pounce on the oncoming Venturas and their close escort.

Nearing the Dutch coast the British force climbed to 12,000 ft. and levelled off in a cloudless sky; but no sooner had it done so than it was suddenly ambushed by four formations of Bf. 109s and Fw. 190s, totalling over 70 aircraft. The Focke-Wulfs went for the Spitfires while the Messerschmitts began to pick off the Venturas one by one. Duffill's machine was one of the first to be hit. Cannon fire destroyed the hydraulic system—preventing the bomb doors from opening properly, among other things—set both engines

alight and wounded the wireless operator. Duffill was forced to retire but before he did so his gunner, Sgt L. Neill, R.A.F., claimed a Fw. 190. In the process Neill, too, was wounded, being almost blown out of his turret.

Two other Venturas of Duffill's formation which followed him were headed off and shot down, but Duffill, although attacked repeatedly until well out over the North Sea, managed to keep his machine airborne. His navigator, F/O F. J. Starkie, R.A.F., did his best to make the two wounded crew members comfortable and then turned his attention to the bombs which were still lodged in the racks and which were a source of danger in the event of a forced landing. He lifted the trap-door and succeeded in releasing three of the bombs, meanwhile keeping his energetic captain cheerful by entering the cockpit after each success and shouting in Duffill's ear: 'I've got another b—— off, sir.' Duffill eventually managed to reach Methwold and land the crippled Ventura safely. It was the only one to return and each member of the crew received an immediate decoration.

As the remaining Venturas flew on towards the target they were attacked repeatedly, and then, when only three remained, an enemy fighter flew across Trent's bows and offered a perfect shot at a range of about 150 yards. 'Had always longed for just such a chance', Trent said afterwards, 'and down he went, for the Ventura's best armament was under the pilot's thumb. I hardly had to move the aircraft.' A Dutch boy, who was then 18, wrote an account of how he witnessed the incident and saw a Bf. 109 crash.

Meanwhile Trent's Number Three had gone down in flames so that Trent and his Number Two, 'who was flying as if it were a practice mission over Norfolk', were the only ones left as the target was neared. Flak bursts suddenly appeared all over the place, the fighters were in no way deterred and appeared to redouble their efforts to add to their score. After what seemed like a lifetime Trent completed his run-in and released his bombs. They overshot but did cause some blast damage to the target.

Trent was now alone and faced with the task of running the gauntlet of the enemy defences back to the coast in order to get home. He closed the bomb doors, but even as he did so his machine was hit; all the flying controls were shot away and the bomber went

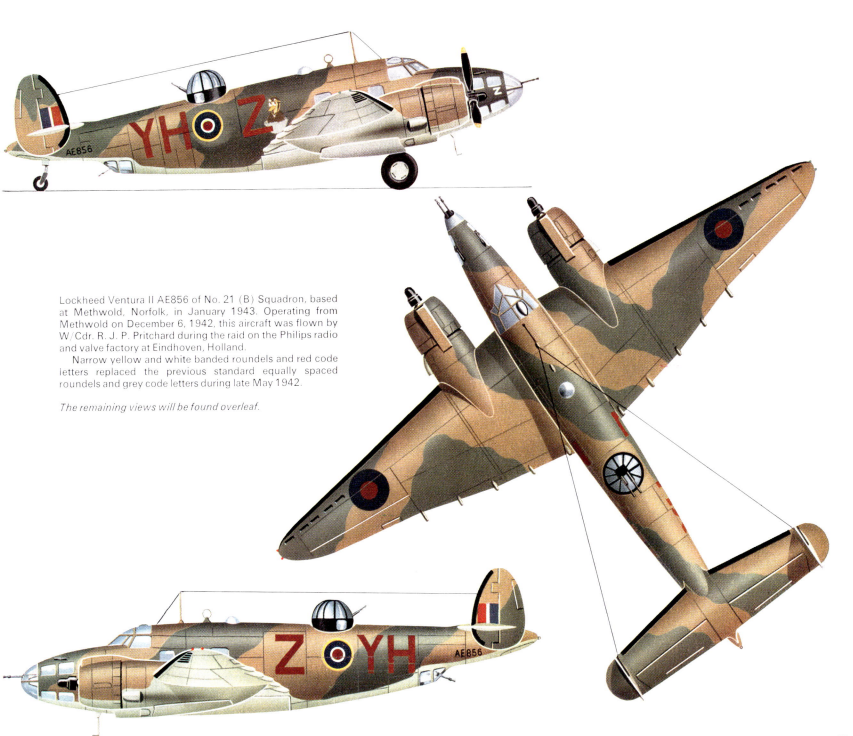

Lockheed Ventura II AE856 of No. 21 (B) Squadron, based at Methwold, Norfolk, in January 1943. Operating from Methwold on December 6, 1942, this aircraft was flown by W/Cdr. R. J. P. Pritchard during the raid on the Philips radio and valve factory at Eindhoven, Holland.

Narrow yellow and white banded roundels and red code letters replaced the previous standard equally spaced roundels and grey code letters during late May 1942.

*The remaining views will be found overleaf.*

HELL'S A-POPPIN!

| 0 | 1 | 2 | 3 | |
|---|---|---|---|---|
| | | | | M. |

| 0 | 5 | 10 | 15 | |
|---|---|---|---|---|
| | | | | FT. |

Lockheed Ventura II AE856 of
No. 21 (B) Squadron.

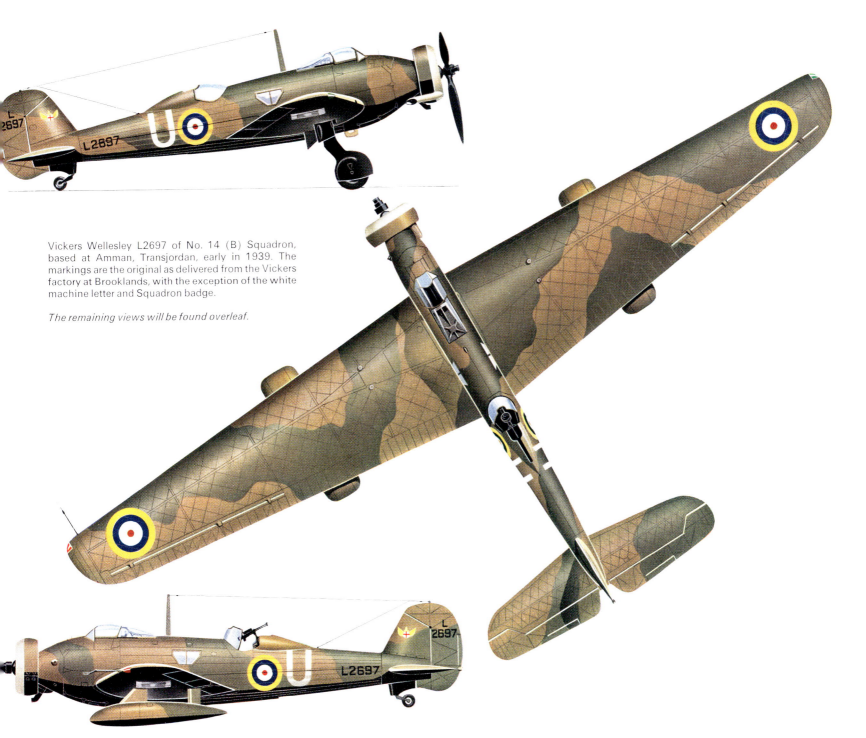

Vickers Wellesley L2697 of No. 14 (B) Squadron, based at Amman, Transjordan, early in 1939. The markings are the original as delivered from the Vickers factory at Brooklands, with the exception of the white machine letter and Squadron badge.

*The remaining views will be found overleaf.*

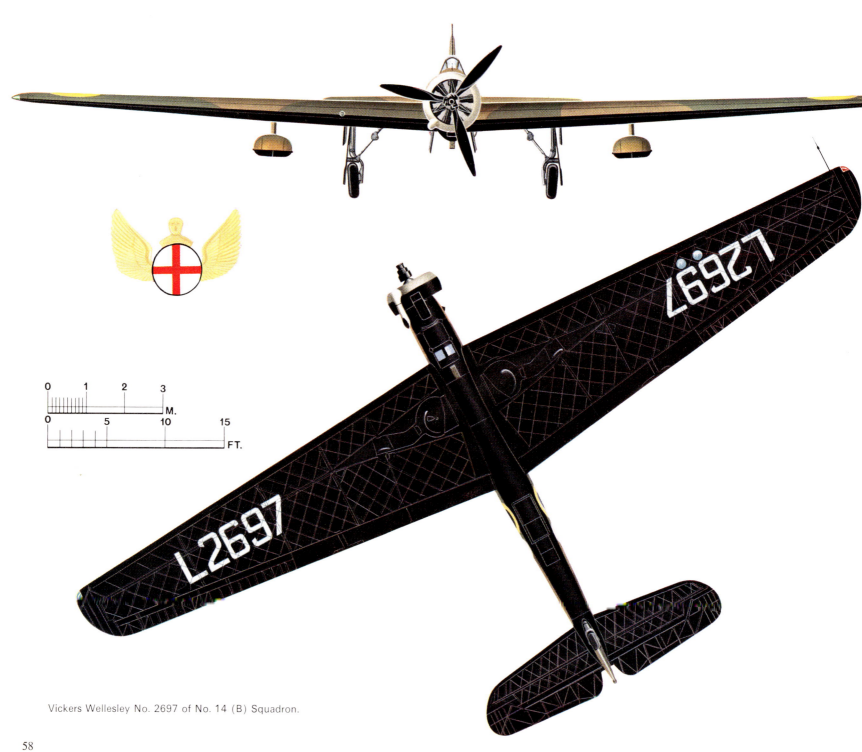

0 1 2 3
M.
0 5 10 15
FT.

Vickers Wellesley No. 2697 of No. 14 (B) Squadron.

down. Trent and his navigator were thrown clear and survived to become prisoners of war, but the other two members of the crew were unable to escape before the Ventura crashed. After the war when the full story of the raid became known S/Ldr Trent was awarded the Victoria Cross.

In June 1943 the 2nd Tactical Air Force was formed in preparation for the invasion of Europe, and 2 Group's Ventura squadrons, together with those flying Bostons and Mitchells, left Bomber Command to join the new force which was, for the time being, to operate under Fighter Command control. 2 Group was now led by A. V. M. Basil Embry and one of the changes that he made in the second half of 1943 was that of raising the maximum bombing height of the 'mediums' to 12,000–14,000 ft. in order to avoid the heavy flak, the actual height being governed by the needs of individual targets and Intelligence reports on their defences.

The Venturas, in common with the other medium bombers, only operated when there was little or no cloud below their bombing altitude, and as a result there were often long intervals between operations. Thus, in June, for example, 21 Squadron flew only three missions, and on one of these—a *Circus* against Abbeville–Drucat airfield on the 22nd, W/Cdr R. H. S. King, the C.O., went missing.

A raid by twelve crews on Mauperthuis airfield, south-east of Paris, on June 24 proved to be 487 Squadron's final operation with Venturas, and in July it moved to Sculthorpe to concentrate on intensive night-flying training prior to re-equipment with Mosquito F.B.VIs. Its last Ventura left on September 21.

464 Squadron also stood down from operations early in July and followed 487 Squadron to Sculthorpe to re-arm with Mosquitoes. 21 Squadron, however, continued operations a little longer, and in August (after an order to convert to Mitchells had been rescinded) the unit was detached to Hartford Bridge (later renamed Blackbushe), Hants, to participate in Operation *Starkey*, a vast combined operation designed to give the appearance of an attempt to seize a bridgehead on the continent of Europe. No. 21's contribution to the simulated invasion—it was a ruse that failed from the air viewpoint as the *Luftwaffe* was never brought to battle as had been hoped—included *Circuses* against the airfield at Triqueville, ammunition dumps at Fôret d'Eperleque and Fôret de Hesdin,

marshalling yards at Abbeville and gun emplacements near Boulogne. The squadron put up eighteen Venturas—three 'boxes' of six for some of these missions, and on one occasion twenty aircraft were despatched. After a final operation on the afternoon of September 9 1943, 21 Squadron stood down, and later in the month it joined 464 and 487 Squadrons at Sculthorpe and began to convert to Mosquitoes. By October 25 it only had one Ventura left on charge and this crashed that same day on proceeding to Bicester, where it overshot on landing and became a total wreck.

## Specification

Ventura I: *Crew* 5; *power plant* two 2,000 h.p. Pratt and Whitney Double Wasp GR2800 S1A4-G; *span* 65 ft. 6 in.; *length* 51 ft. 5 in.; *wing area* 551 sq. ft.; *empty weight* 17,275 lb.; *loaded weight* 27,250 lb.; *max. bomb load* 2,500 lb.; *max. speed* 315 m.p.h. at 15,500 ft.; *service ceiling* 25,000 ft.; *range* 925 miles with max. bomb load; *armament* two fixed forward-firing .50 in. m.g. and two depressable .303 in. m.g. in nose, two or four .303 in. m.g. in dorsal turret, and two .303 m.g. in ventral position.

*Seven feet of the wing of this Ventura were shorn off on a strafing run over the German-occupied Lowlands but the aircraft managed to fly safely back to base.*

# Vickers Wellesley

In 1931 the Air Ministry issued a specification for a general-purpose aircraft of outstanding versatility, its intended roles ranging from light bombing and photography to casualty evacuation and torpedo-bombing. Among the many offerings were two from Vickers—one for a biplane and the other for a monoplane. Both designs utilised the goedetic system of construction which had been perfected by Dr. Barnes Wallis and first employed in the airship *R-100*. This system was based on the theory that the shortest distance between two points on a curved surface is a geodetic line. Thus the bracing members were not placed vertically and horizontally in the sides and top and bottom panels of a fuselage, but ran diagonally around the fuselage, forming two or more spirals of opposite direction. All these criss-crossing members were self-supporting, so, instead of pulling or squashing them, any load which tried to force one set of members inwards or outwards was automatically cancelled out by an equal and opposite force in the intersecting set. The system dispensed with stressed-skin covering and fabric covering was used.

The Air Ministry ordered a prototype of the Vickers general-purpose biplane for evaluation. This machine,

K2771, first flew in August 1934 and did well enough in A. & A.E.E. trials to prompt an order for 150 production examples for the R.A.F. Meanwhile, Vickers were so convinced of the superiority of the alternative monoplane design that they decided to build it as a private venture. The resulting prototype, K7556, made its maiden flight on June 19 1935, and proved to have such a vastly improved performance that the Air Ministry was persuaded to switch the order from the biplane to the monoplane. Thus in September 1935 the biplane order was cancelled and replaced with a contract for 79 monoplanes, the first of which began to enter service with Bomber Command in the spring of 1937 as the Wellesley. Later a further 97 Wellesleys were ordered, the 176th and last machine being delivered in May 1938.

First squadron to receive the Wellesley was the newly-formed No. 76, at Finningley, Yorks, in April 1937. Four more Bomber Command squadrons—Nos. 35, 77, 148 and 207—subsequently received Wellesleys, but by the outbreak of war the type had

been almost completely withdrawn from Bomber Command service,* and 118 had been transferred fo service in the Middle East.

Four squadrons flew Wellesleys in the Middle East —Nos. 14, 47, 45 and 223. First to be equipped wa No. 45 at Helwan, Egypt, which received its first machine on November 25 1937. This squadron moved to Ismailia in January 1939 and in June of that year converted to Blenheim Is. The other units were al flying Wellesleys at the outbreak of World War II, and when Italy entered the war in June 1940, they were all based in the Sudan—No. 14 at Port Sudan, No. 4 at Erkowit and No. 223 at Summit.

On the first day of the East African campaign, 14 Squadron made a highly successful attack on Massawa probably its most famous operation of the war Bombing-up started at dawn but owing to trouble with the Wellesleys' underwing bomb containers it was no completed until midday. It was therefore decided to hit Massawa at dusk. Nine aircraft, led by the C.O. S/Ldr A. D. Selway (now A.V.M. Selway) took part

*Wellesley K7725 of 76 Squadron on a flight from its base at Finningley in July 1937. ['Aeroplane'.*

* Only Bomber Command squadron with Wellesleys still o charge was No. 76, then serving as an O.T.U.

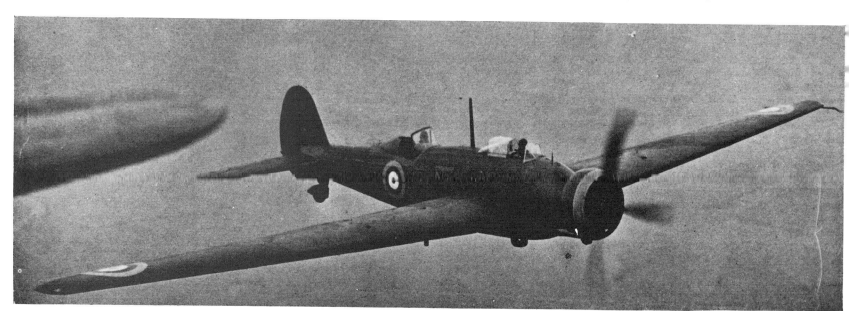

he first two sections of three bombing from 600 ft.
The C.O.'s second salvo, a mixture of 40-lb. and
0-lb. high-explosive bombs and incendiaries, des-
royed a bulk fuel installation in the harbour, setting it
light, while the other five machines, following at
00 ft. and carrying similar loads, scored direct hits on
angars and other buildings at Otumlo airfield and
tarted another fire. The third section, carrying
50-pounders, followed at 3,500 ft. and succeeded in
coring a direct hit on a hangar; they also bombed a
ailway. It was learned afterwards that the C.O.'s
ombs sent 780 tons of fuel up in flames. For the
ecord, the machines that took part in this attack—
vhich was made without loss—were L2647 (S/Ldr
elway), K7225, L2645, L2652, K7741, K7723, L2649
nd L2710.

From then on No. 14 made frequent raids on
Massawa in addition to attacking other objectives in
Eritrea such as the airfields at Gura and Asmara.
Normal armament of the Wellesley comprised a
Vickers gun forward and one Vickers K gun aft, but
his was augmented in the case of No. 14's machines
by a ventral K gun on mountings of the squadron's own
design. Thus on June 26, when No. 14's Wellesleys
oined those of 47 Squadron in a raid on Gura, the
ormer flew at a lower level to afford protection from
attacks from below. Seven Fiat C.R.42s attacked the
ormation, and although they failed to shoot any of
he bombers down, they did succeed in holing the fuel
anks of S/Ldr Selway's machine, flooding the floor
vith petrol, with the result that for most of the way
ome Selway was forced to lean out of the cockpit to
avoid asphyxiation. Two more of No. 14's machines
vere slightly damaged by the C.R.42s, but on the
credit side one of the enemy fighters was driven off
vith smoke pouring from it, while another appeared
o go down out of control.

On July 8, 'B' Flight's Wellesleys operated for the
irst time with three rear guns fitted; in addition to the
under-gun already mentioned, twin guns were installed
n the rear gunner's cockpit—again on mountings of
No. 14's own design—in place of the standard single
novable gun installation. These enabled the mid-upper
gunner to fire through an arc from the forward quarter
o the rear quarter. On this first mission with the new
armament the formation of five Wellesleys encoun-
ered, during the return journey, an S.M.81, which had
apparently been searching for a British convoy.
F/O G. S. R. Robinson, the leader, flying in K7723,
broke up his formation, and after attacking the enemy
bomber from astern and quarter, saw it crash into the
sea and break up.

To make their raids, the ageing Wellesleys had to

Line up of Wellesleys of 148 Squadron at Scampton in 1938. On September 29 that year K7732 crashed and killed its crew of three at Kedington, near Stradishall, when a wing broke off following a dive through rain-cloud.

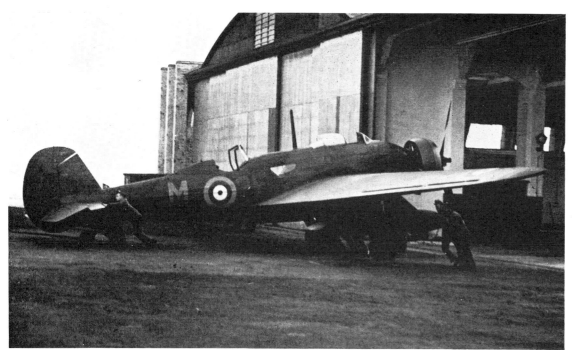

*K8526 ('M-Mother' of 35 Squadron is pushed from its hangar at Worthy Down in 1937 or 1938.*

fly across what was some of the most dangerous flying country in the world—country where forced landings were out of the question and where the natives were unfriendly to the point of murder. Added to these hazards were the Italian flak and fighters, and many a time machines struggled home looking like colanders, to crash-land on the sandy airfield at Port Sudan. If a Wellesley was winged and lagged behind, the waiting enemy fighters would close in and give it hell. This happened on July 16 to a young squadron leader who, after having 'flown a desk' for several months had asked to take part in a raid on warships at Massawa to relieve the boredom. He was given the job of rear gunner and his guns were blown away. The pilot was hit, and the under-gunner mortally wounded. The squadron leader fixed a tourniquet, tightened it with his revolver, and got the dying airman to hold it in place. Eventually the pilot, lacking blood, could control the striken bomber no longer so the squadron leader took over. The Wellesley got home but by then the wounded under-gunner was dead.

By the end of August, in nearly three months of operations against the Italians in East Africa, No. 14 Squadron had made 22 bombing raids, each of 6 hr. 10 min. average duration, and dropped 43 tons of bombs of all types—but mainly 250-pounders. Two Wellesleys were lost over enemy territory. The squadron began to rearm with Blenheim IVs in mid-September and eventually the Wellesleys were transferred to Nos. 47 and 223 Squadrons.

No. 47 Squadron, in the months which preceded Italy's entry into the war, was engaged, like the other Wellesley units, in routine patrols. It was based at Khartoum at that time but moved in May 1940 to Erkowit, in the Red Sea hills. Its first wartime bombing mission—against the airfield at Asmara, the Eritrean capital—was made on June 11. A move was made to Carthago in July and during the few months more raids were made on Italian airfields, particularly those at Azoza and Gondar. Sometimes the enemy retaliated. On October 16, eight of his aircraft swept down on Gedaref airfield, where eight 47 Squadron Wellesleys were parked, and reduced the Wellesleys to blazing wrecks.

In November a detachment operated from Khartoum

*Another view of a Wellesley being removed from its hangar—this time a 14 Squadron aircraft, L2661, at Amman, Palestine, before World War II. Note the cut-out for the gun in the rear cockpit canopy fairing. [I.W.M.*

nd at the end of the month the squadron head-
quarters moved there, with detachments at Kassala
nd Argordat carrying out photographic reconnais-
ance and strikes on enemy gun positions and troop
oncentrations. When the Italians capitulated in
Abyssinia in May 1941 the squadron took over Asmara
irfield.

During its stay at Asmara, No. 47 was engaged in
ropping supplies to our armed forces at Debarech
ntil the fall of Gondar on November 28 1941, when
he war in East Africa ended. At the end of the year the
quadron left the Sudan for Egypt to re-equip with
eauforts, only to find on arrival that all the new
ircraft had been allocated to another unit. Eventually
ome old Wellesleys were rejuvenated, and these
iven to 47 Squadron Air Echelon, which was formed
n April 16 1942, and first located at Burg el Arab,
ter moving to Shandur and St. Jean. The Wellesleys
ew convoy patrols off the Nile Delta area and the
oast of Palestine until the end of February 1943,
hen the echelon was disbanded.

The third Wellesley squadron in the Middle East at
he outbreak of war, No. 223, was transferred in June
940 from the Sudan to Aden, and on August 18—
he day on which our troops were being withdrawn
om British Somaliland—five of its machines set off
om an advanced base at Perim Island for Addis
baba. 'The enemy capital' states the Short Official
listory, 'had thus far been neither reconnoitred nor
ttacked. By a brilliant feat of airmanship, four of the
ircraft now forced their way over wickedly mountain-
us country and through heavy cloud and ice to bomb
he airfields outside the town. Despite severe damage
om anti-aircraft fire and the opposition of one
enacious C.R.32 all four Wellesleys returned safely to
ase; so too, did the fifth, which became lost, landed
o find itself in French Somaliland and took off again
while the French authorities were looking up their
egulations. The four pilots who reached their objective
rought back with them excellent photographs and
he satisfaction of having destroyed four S.M.79s,
hree hangars and the Duke of Iosta's private aircraft.'

From the outset of the East African campaign, 223
quadron operated against Italian installations in the
Red Sea coastal area. Petrol dumps and workshops at
Gura and the port of Massawa were bombed and
xcellent results achieved. The squadron also struck

at the enemy airfield at Tessenei, destroying hangars
and aircraft on the ground. During this period attacks
were also made on communications and airfields in
Somaliland.

Early in 1941 raids were made in support of the
Army's drive into Eritrea. Enemy airfields and troop
concentrations were bombed and, where possible,
support was also given to Abyssinian patriots who,
encouraged by our air attacks, stepped up their own
activities which harassed the retreating Italians still
further.

Early in April 1941, when the battle for Eritrea
had been won, 223 Squadron was posted to Shandur,
Egypt, to rearm with Martin Marylands, but before
leaving East Africa it received praise in the A.O.C.-in-
C.'s official despatch for the work it had accomplished
there with only a handful of obsolescent Wellesleys.

## Specification

Wellesley: *Crew* 2; *power plant* one 925 h.p. Bristol
Pegasus XX; *span* 74 ft. 7 in.; *length* 39 ft. 3 in.; *wing
area* 630 sq. ft.; *empty weight* 6,369 lb.; *loaded weight*
11,100 lb.; *max. bomb load* 2,000 lb; *max. speed*
228 m.p.h. at 19,680 ft.; *service ceiling* 33,000 ft.;
*max. range* 1,000 miles with 1,060 lb. bombs; *armament* one fixed .303 in. m.g. forward, one .303 in. m.g.
in dorsal position (sometimes one extra dorsal .303 in.
m.g. and/or a ventral .303 in. m.g. was fitted).

Above: Wellesleys, including K7777, nearest camera, lined up on an airfield in Egypt before World War II.

Below: K7742 'T-Tommy' of 45 Squadron pictured over the old airship mooring mast at Heliopolis, Egypt, early in 1939. [Charles E. Brown.